COMPUTERS OUR LIFELINE

4

Based on NEP

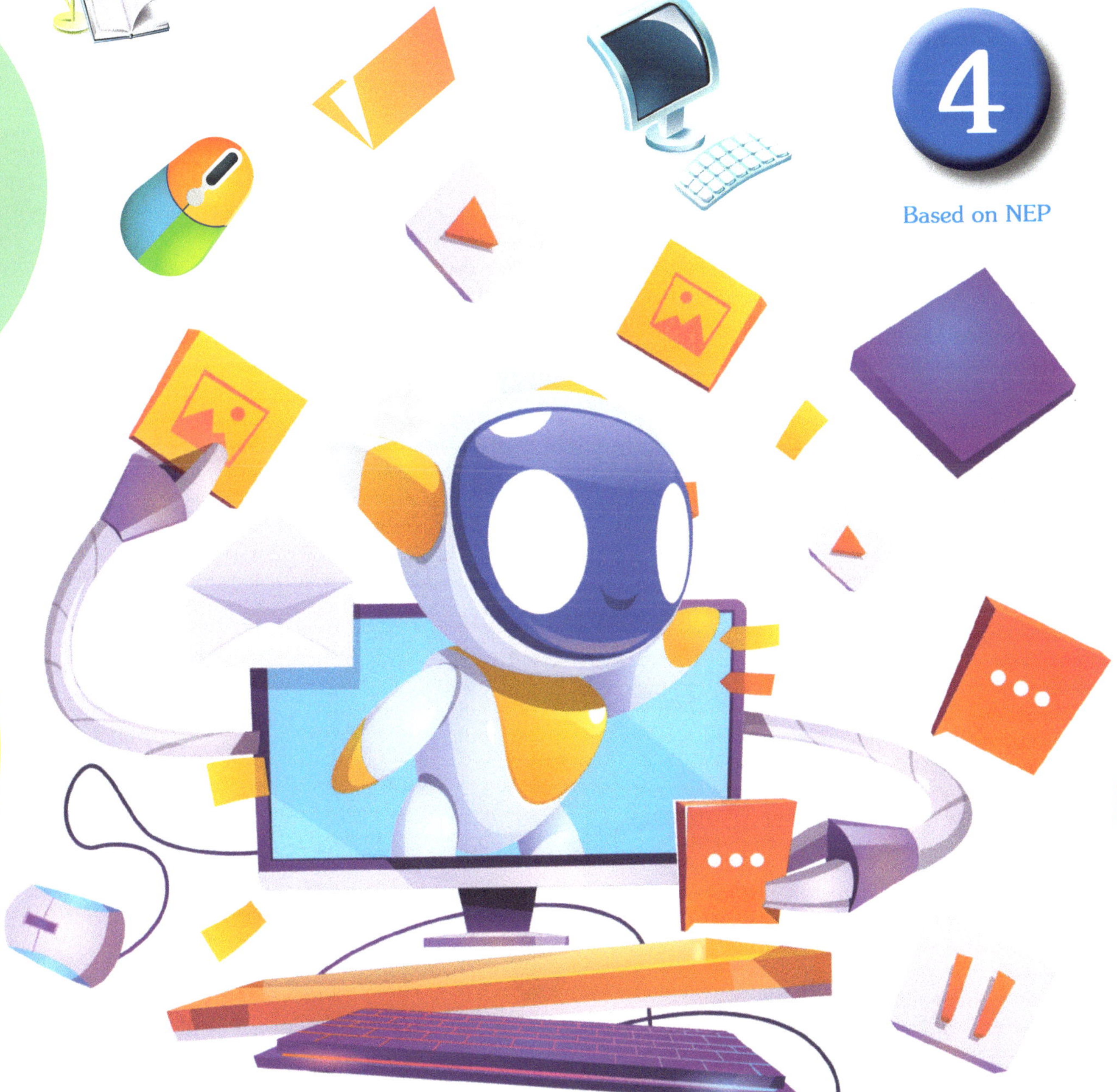

MANOJ PUBLICATIONS

COMPUTERS
Our Lifeline - 4

Publishers:

MANOJ PUBLICATIONS

761, Main Road, Burari, Delhi-110084 (INDIA)

Mobile : 09999476076, 09868112194,
08178823569, 08178854810

Email : info@manojpublications.com

For online shopping visit our website :

Website : www.sawanonlinebookstore.com

ISBN : 978-81-310-1642-8

Concept:

Puneet Gupta

M.B.A. (William & Mary, U.S.A.)

Edited by:

Davinder Singh Minhas

Rohan Kumar

PREFACE

This is the Age of Computers. In every nook and corner of the globe, computers have made their presence felt, be it school, office, post office, bank, shop, mall, hotel, restaurant, airport, railway station, Metro station and so on. Needless to say, they have become our lifeline as we can't do anything without them. In order to keep pace with the modern world, it is important to familiarise our children with computer applications right from the start. They ought to be taught the uses of computer in a lucid, interesting and enjoyable style: from basic to intermediate to advanced level.

Keeping in view the requirements of students, all the books in the series—Computers : Our Lifeline—have been designed to meet the purpose of acquiring a sound in-depth knowledge on computers with their uses. The contents of the books are based entirely on recently approved NEP (National Educational Policy).

The chapters in all the books contain a fairly good amount of illustrations which make the text very easy to understand. There are many computer books flooding the market. Our books are the books with a difference in order that they are well equipped with exhaustive exercises which test a student's mental horizon by making him take Formative Assessment as well as Summative Assessment. The knowledge of the latest software with their applications and types of computer language have been made available. Nay, students have been introduced to coding, the process of designing computer apps. The main goal of books in the series is to make a student computerate, *i.e.* computer literate.

We sincerely hope that all the books in this series will prove fruitful both to students and teachers. We shall be highly pleased to receive constructive suggestions in order to make the series more qualitative in the forthcoming editions.

– Author

CONTENTS

1 Computer: Its History

Hello friends! I am back here again to tell you more about the computer. Do you know where the computer has come from? The computer which you are using today, was not like this before. It took many years to make the computer. Let me take you to the history of the computer. Come and join me.

EVOLUTION OF COMPUTER

The computer is a combination of ideas and talent of people, from across the world. Organizations and individuals have worked together for many years to make the computer the valuable machine that has brought about a revolution in the world of technology.

Today the computer has become the important part of our life and it has made our life very fast and easy. It is a versatile machine that can do arithmetic as well as non-arithmetic calculations. The concept of counting started with the existence of human beings.

Earlier, people were dependent on stones, pebbles, bones, sticks, etc. for counting. They used to mark on walls, pillars, stones, etc. for recording information.

Stones

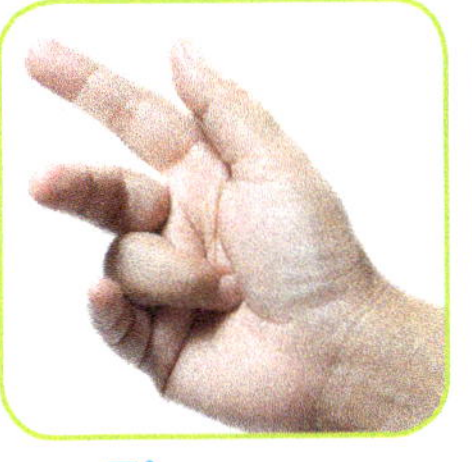

Sticks

Fingers

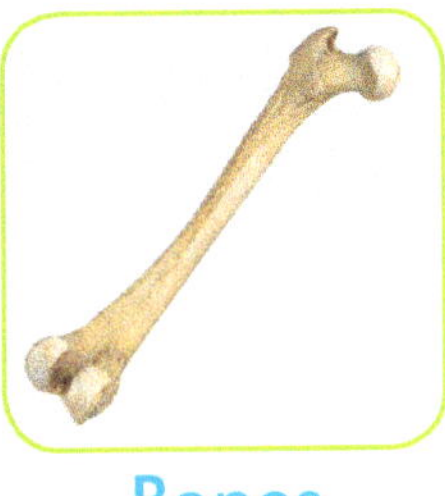

Bones

Pebbles

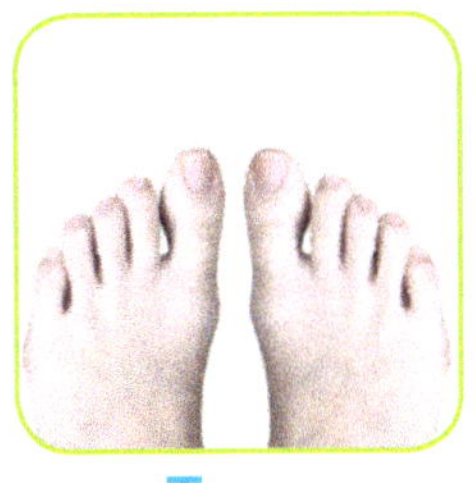

Toes

As the time advanced, doing bigger and complex calculations with such objects became difficult. They had their own limitations. Therefore, the need for different devices felt for the same and the first calculating device 'ABACUS' was invented.

Abacus

Abacus was the first mechanical device developed about 5000 years ago in China. It has a wooden frame that consists of wires and beads. These beads are used for doing simple calculations like addition and subtraction. It is still in use in some parts of China. It is also known as counting frame.

Do you know ?

- *The abacus is also used in pre-schools as an aid in teaching the numeral system.*
- *The user of an abacus is called an abacist.*
- *In India the knowledge and use of an abacus was described by Abhidharmakosa.*

Napier's Bones

Napier's bones was a calculating device created by John Napier in 1617. It consisted of a wooden box that had strips of wood or carved bones on which the multiplication tables were inscribed. The Multiplication was reduced by Napier's bones to a sequence of simple additions. Napier's bones was also used for addition, subtraction, multiplication and division of numbers.

John Napier

Napier's Bones

Pascaline

Blaise Pascal invented a mechanical device for adding and subtracting numbers in 1642. It is known as Pascal's Arithmetic Machine or Pascaline. Pascal developed the device in order to help his father in his work. The machine had a set of eight movable gears that worked together to do calculations like addition and subtraction.

Blaise Pascal

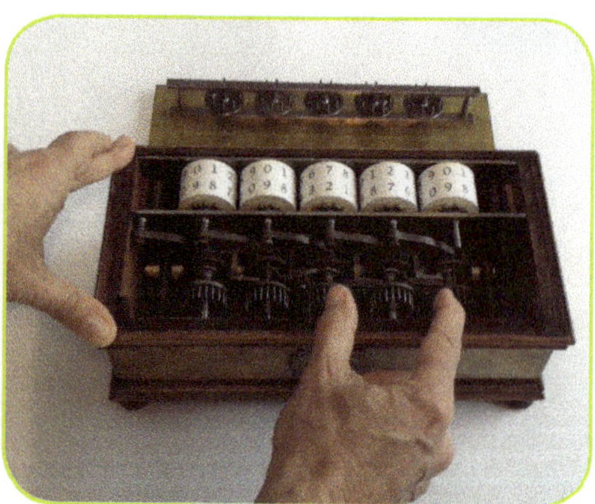

Pascaline

Jacquard's Loom

In 1804, Joseph Jacquard of France invented a new type of loom for weaving cloth. Punched cards were used to control the operation of the loom. His idea of using punched cards to store information was used by a number of computer inventors in later years.

Jacquard Loom on display at Museum of Science and Industry in Manchester, England

Babbage's Analytical Engine

Perhaps the first calculating machine that can be truly called a computer was invented in England by Charles Babbage in 1837. Babbage's dream was to build a machine that could do more than just calculate big numbers. It would receive instructions, process and store information and finally print the results. He planned to call it the Analytical Engine. Furthermore, only some part of the machine was constructed due to lack of funds. Then Babbage's colleague and close friend, Lady Augusta Ada Lovelace, helped him to complete the machine.

Charles Babbage is also known as the Father of Computers as he invented the machine with the features on which today's modern computer works.

Analytical Engine

Charles Babbage

Lady Augusta Ada Lovelace

Lady Augusta Ada Lovelace is best known as the 'first programmer' of computer language.

Tabulating Machine

Herman Hollerith

In 1890, another important machine was built by an army engineer Herman Hollerith. This machine was called Tabulating Machine. Hollerith borrowed the idea of the punched card from a French weaver, Joseph Jacquard.

The Tabulating Machine was used in Census to count the population of the USA. It gave a 'quick' count of the U.S. population. The use of the Tabulating Machine was so successful that Hollerith formed a company that later became famous as the International Business Machine or IBM.

Hollerith's Tabulating Machine

Do you know ?

Census means the counting of the people in a particular country.

Mark-I

Howard Aiken

Howard Aiken, An American engineer at Harvard University, built the first Electro Mechanical Computer named Mark-I in 1944. Mark-I worked very much like a machine designed more than a 100 years earlier (Babbage's Analytical Engine).

Mark-I was the first computer in real sense. It was 51 feet long, weighed 5 ton and used punched cards and typewriter for input and output. Today Mark-I is considered to be "the beginning of the era of the modern computer."

Mark-I

ENIAC

ENIAC (Electronic Numerical Integrator And Computer) was designed by John Eckert and John Mauchly at the University of Pennsylvania in Philadelphia. It was the first large-scale, electronic digital computer capable of being reprogrammed to solve a full range of computing problems.

ENIAC was started in 1942 and completed in 1945. It was decimal-based, used 18,000 vacuum tubes, took up 1,800 square feet and performed 5,000 additions/second. Today, the equivalent technology fits in a wrist-watch.

ENIAC

Jean Bartik was the first ENIAC computer programmer.

UNIVAC

UNIVAC (Universal Automatic Computer) was the first commercially successful computer introduced in 1951 by Remington Rand. It was designed by J. Presper Eckert and John Mauchly, also the inventors of ENIAC (the first fully electronic computer).

UNIVAC was the first computer to handle both numeric and textual information. It had three different times—an add time of 120 microseconds, multiply time of 1,800 microseconds and a divide time of 3,600 microseconds.

UNIVAC

J. Presper and John Mauchly

PC-AT

After covering the long way, the IBM introduced the first Personal Computer called PC–AT (Personal Computer Advanced Technology) in 1981. These computers were small in size, fast in speed and accurate.

Today, several types of PC are available like desktop computer, laptop computer and palmtop.

IBM PC

LET'S HAVE A LOOK

- Earlier people were dependent on stones, pebbles, bones, sticks, etc. for counting.
- The first calculating device is Abacus.
- John Napier had invented the Napier's Bones.
- The Pascaline was invented by Blaise Pascal in 1642.
- Joseph Marie Jacquard invented the Jacquard loom in 1804.
- The Analytical Engine was developed by Charles Babbage.
- Charles Babbage is called the Father of Computers.
- The world's first programmer is Lady Augusta Ada Lovelace.
- The Hollerith's adding machine was invented by Herman Hollerith.
- The MARK-1 series of computers was designed by Howard Aiken and Grace Hopper at Harvard University.
- John Mauchly and J. Presper Eckert developed the ENIAC in 1946.
- A computer milestone, named UNIVAC, was achieved by Dr. Presper Eckert and Dr. John Mauchly, the team which invented the ENIAC computer.

BRAIN TEASER

1. Answer each of the following in one word or line:

a. Name the first calculating machine.

____

b. Name the machine invented by Charles Babbage.

____

c. What did the early man use for calculations?

____

d. Who invented the Analytical Engine?

____

e. Name the first full-electronic computer.

____

f. Name the two devices developed by John Presper Eckert and John Mauchly.

____

2. Answer the following questions:

a. What is an abacus?

b. What were the contributions of John Napier and Blaise Pascal to the field of the computer?

c. Why is Charles Babbage called the Father of Computers?

d. Who is known as the 'first programmer' of the computer?

e. Describe ENIAC and UNIVAC.

f. What is PC-AT?

3. Write short notes on the following:

a. Abacus

b. Mark-I

c. UNIVAC

d. Analytical Engine

4. Write 'T' for true and 'F' for false in the boxes:

a. The Analytical Engine was invented by Charles Jones. ☐

b. The Abacus was invented by Augusta Ada. ☐

c. Howard Aiken designed the MARK-I series. ☐

d. MARK-I is the first generation computer. ☐

e. Pascaline was developed by Blaise Pascal. ☐

f. PC-AT was developed by IBM. ☐

5. Multiple Choice Questions

Tick (✓) the correct answer:

a. The first calculating device made in China

i. Mark-I ☐ ii. Pascaline ☐ iii. Abacus ☐

b. The early man used to count on

i. Calculator ☐ ii. Computer ☐ iii. Stones ☐

c. The Pascaline was invented by Blaise Pascal in

i. 1645 ☐ ii. 1642 ☐ iii. 1617 ☐

d. The first ENIAC computer programmer

i. John Mauchly ☐ ii. Jean Bartik ☐ iii. Howard Aiken ☐

e. The Analytical Engine was invented by

i. John Napier ☐ ii. Gottfried ☐ iii. Charles Babbage ☐

f. The Father of Computers is

i. John Mauchly ☐ ii. Blaise Pascal ☐ iii. Charles Babbage ☐

6. Fill in the blanks:

a. The Abacus was invented in ____________ 5000 years ago.

b. John Napier invented a calculating device called the ____________.

c. ____________________________ is known as the Father of computers.

d. ___________________ was specially designed to count the US Census.

e. _________________________ was the first electro-mechanical computer.

f. PC-AT was introduced by ____________________________ in 1981.

7. Match the following:

a.	Analytical Engine	i.	Howard Aiken
b.	Tabulating machine	ii.	IBM
c.	Pascaline	iii.	Charles Babbage
d.	Mark-I	iv.	UNIVAC
e.	Remington Rand	v.	Census
f.	PC-AT	vi.	Blaise Pascal

8. Write the years and the inventors of the following:

		Year	Inventor
a.	Analytical Engine	______	______
b.	Pascaline	______	______
c.	Mark-I	______	______
d.	Tabulating Machine	______	______
e.	UNIVAC	______	______
f.	PC-AT	______	______

Draw the Chinese Abacus and PC-AT below and write two differences between them.

ABACUS	PC-AT

2 Types Of Computers

Hello! In the previous chapter, you learnt about the origin of computers.

In this lesson, we shall study about different types of computers that have been developed with different designs and features. Some computers have very high capacity as well as working speed; however, some are slow. Depending upon the requirements, computers are being developed.

TYPES OF COMPUTERS

The computer is an electronic machine that performs different types of tasks very quickly and efficiently. It is used in many places like in a computer lab or at home. You must have noticed computers in different shapes, sizes and weights. These different computers also perform different sorts of tasks.

The term microcomputer is synonymous with the personal computer or that which depends on a microprocessor. A microcomputer is small but very powerful. But its power is not sufficient for large organizations. Computers can be classified according to their sizes, processing speeds and costs.

We can divide computers into three types, based on the type of data they are designed to process. These are:

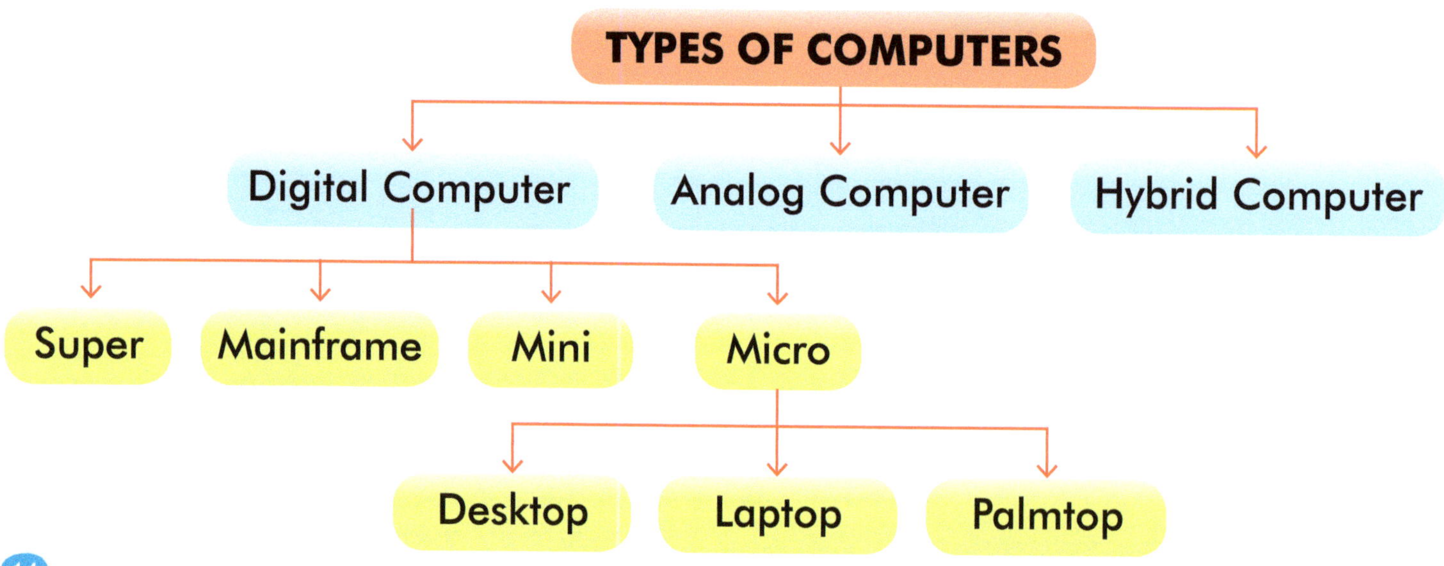

DIGITAL COMPUTER

⇒ The computers which work in binary digits (0 and 1) are known as Digital computers. These digits help carry out all the operations.

⇒ The digital computer is designed using digital circuits that can give more accurate and faster results.

⇒ The digital computer is well suited for solving complex problems in engineering and technology. Hence digital computers have an increasing use in the fields of design, research and data processing.

Desktop computers, Laptops, Calculators, Digital wrist-watches etc., are the devices that work on digital data.

Micro Computer

Laptop

Digital wrist-watch

Calculator

There are four different types of digital computers when we classify them based on their performance and capacity. The four types are Super computer, Mainframe computer, Mini computer and Micro computer.

Super Computer

→ The Super Computer is the largest, fastest and most expensive computer available. It can carry out trillions of operations per second.

⇒ Super Computers are mainly used for the heavy stuffs like weather forecasting, launching satellites, designing the wings of supersonic aircraft, etc. All these require extensive calculations to solve which is possible in Super computers only.

⇒ The examples of Super computers are: CRAY-MP/14, PARAM and ANURAG which are being manufactured in India.

Super Computer

Mainframe Computer

⇒ The large computer, manufactured by IBM, has got the industry term 'Mainframe.'

⇒ These computer systems are very powerful and expensive and cater for the requirements of several hundred users simultaneously at remote terminals.

⇒ The processing speed of the Mainframe computer is in the range of hundreds of million instructions/second.

⇒ Some of the applications of Mainframe computers are broadcasting, airline booking systems, sales systems, advertising, centralized payroll systems and large integrated production planning and control systems.

⇒ The examples of Mainframe computers are IBM 360, 3090 and CDC 6600.

Mainframe

Do you know ?

The mainframe computer was first developed by IBM.

Mini Computer

⇒ Mini computers are lower than mainframe computers in terms of speed and storage capacity. Mini computers are also called Workstations.

⇒ Mini computers are also less expensive than Mainframe computers.

⇒ Mini computers were introduced in the early 1960s.

Mini Computer

⇒ Mini computers are multiuser computers. More than one person can work on a mini computer at the same time.

⇒ Mini computers are usually used by medium sized businesses and in university department handling database.

Do you know ?

Mini computers announced the new era in computing.

Micro Computer

- ⇒ Micro computer is also known as Personal Computer. It is used by a single person at a time.
- ⇒ It comprises three things—microprocessor chip as CPU, semiconductor ROM for storing programs and a RAM for data.
- ⇒ Micro computers are used for both general purpose computations and manipulations.
- ⇒ We can see personal computers almost in every office, school, shop, etc.
- ⇒ The examples of micro computers are IBM PCs and Apple Mac.

Micro computers are further classified as:

Desktop Computer

Micro computers that we use in our schools and at home are desktop computers. A desktop computer usually sits at one place on a desk or table and is plugged into a wall outlet for power.

It generally has a system unit that contains CPU, hard disk, CD drive, etc.

These computers are normally used by single uses for their word processing and other small application requirements.

Desktop Computer

Laptop

A computer which is portable is known as laptop. It is named so because it can easily fit in one's lap. Laptops work with chargeable batteries. These are very light in weight.

On the screen of a laptop, Liquid Crystal Display [LCD] is used. Laptops are also called as Notebook computers because of their small size.

Laptop

Palmtop

Palmtops are pocket-sized computers. A palmtop is named so because it can easily fit in one's palm. Palmtops are less powerful than laptops and desktop computers. They consist of phone directories and calendars and are capable of calculating. In palmtops, only a few applications are supported. Palmtops are often called hand-held computers or PDAs (Personal Digital Assistants).

Palmtop

ANALOG COMPUTER

⇒ In Analog computers, physical quantities such as voltage, pressure, temperature, speed, etc., are used.

⇒ The results given by analog computers will only be approximate since they deal with quantities that vary continuously.

⇒ Analog computers are less accurate than digital computers.

⇒ Some examples of analog computers are clinical thermometer, voltmeter, speedometer, fuel gauge and scale machine.

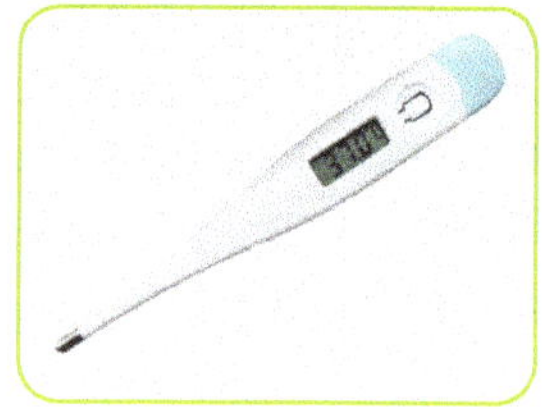

Thermometer

Voltmeter

Speedometer

Fuel gauge

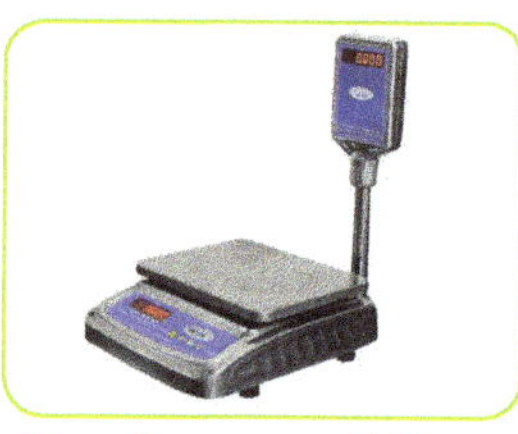

Scale machine

HYBRID COMPUTER

⇒ The computer which uses the capabilities of both digital computer and analog computer is known as hybrid computer.

⇒ We use hybrid computers in weather forecasting and in hospitals where the analog part takes care of the patient's heartbeat and blood pressure. Also, the digital aspects of hybrid computers consider the vital signs during an operation.

⇒ An example of a hybrid computer is ECG machine used in a hospital to measure the heartbeat of the patient.

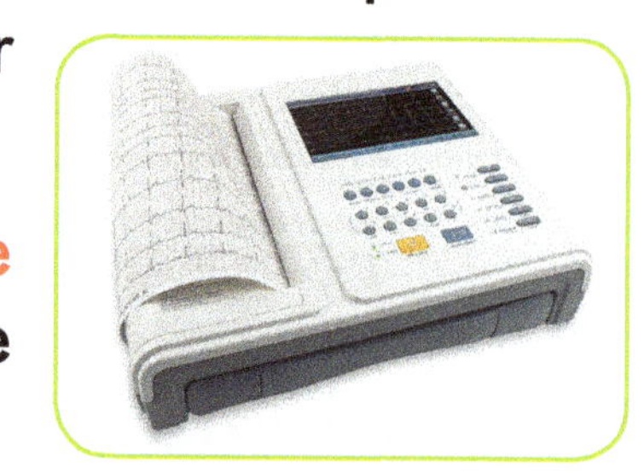

ECG Machine

LET'S HAVE A LOOK

- The computer is an electronic machine that performs different types of tasks very quickly and efficiently.
- The term micro computer is synonymous with personal computer or that which depends on a microprocessor.
- Digital, Analog and Hybrid are the three main types of computers.
- The computers which work in binary digits (0 and 1) are known as Digital computers.
- The four types of digital computers are Super computer, Mainframe computer, Minicomputer and Micro computer.
- The Super computer is the largest, fastest and most expensive computer available.
- The large computer, manufactured by IBM, has got the industry term 'Mainframe'.
- Mini computers are also called Workstations.
- The Micro computer is also known as Personal computer.
- Micro computers that we use in our schools and at home are desktop computers.
- A computer which is portable is known as a laptop.
- Palmtops are often called hand-held computers or PDAs.
- The computer which uses the capabilities of both digital computer and analog computer is known as hybrid computer.

BRAIN TEASER

1. Answer each of the following in one word or line:

a. Name the three categories of the computer.

____

b. Name the computer used for weather forecasting.

____

c. What is the other name for a mini computer?

____

d. Name the computer designed for a single user.

____

e. Name the computer that uses the capabilities of both digital computer and analog computer.

____

2. Answer the following questions:

a. Define a micro computer.

b. Which is the largest and fastest computer ever made? Explain briefly.

c. What are the uses of a mainframe computer?

d. Write the difference between an analog and a digital computer.

e. What is the use of a hybrid computer?

3. Multiple Choice Questions

Tick (✓) the correct answer:

a. The computer which works in binary digits (0 and 1) is

i. Digital ☐ ii. Analog ☐ iii. Micro ☐

b. A combination of analog and digital computer

i. Hybrid ☐ ii. Mini ☐

iii. General purpose ☐

c. The computer used by a single person at a time

i. Mini ☐ ii. Mainframe ☐ iii. Micro ☐

d. Which one is the portable computer?

i. Analog Computer ☐ ii. Laptop ☐ iii. Palmtop ☐

e. Which one is the example of a micro computer?

i. Speedometer ☐ ii. IBM PC ☐ iii. Hybrid ☐

4. Match the following:

a. Micro Computer	i. less accurate than digital computer
b. Palmtop	ii. fastest computer ever made
c. Mini Computer	iii. developed by IBM
d. Super Computer	iv. used for computations and manipulations
e. Analog Computer	v. workstation
f. Mainframe Computer	vi. pocket-sized computer

5. Number the following types of computers from big to small, based on their physical shapes.

Micro Computer

Mainframe

Super Computer

Laptop

Palmtop

ACTIVITY TIME

Collect the pictures of mainframe, mini computer, micro computer, laptop and palmtop from newspapers or magazines and paste them in your activity-book.

Formative Assessment-1
(Chapters 1-2)

1. Match the following devices with their inventors:

a. 

b. 

c. 

d. 

e. 

f. 

2. Complete the following:

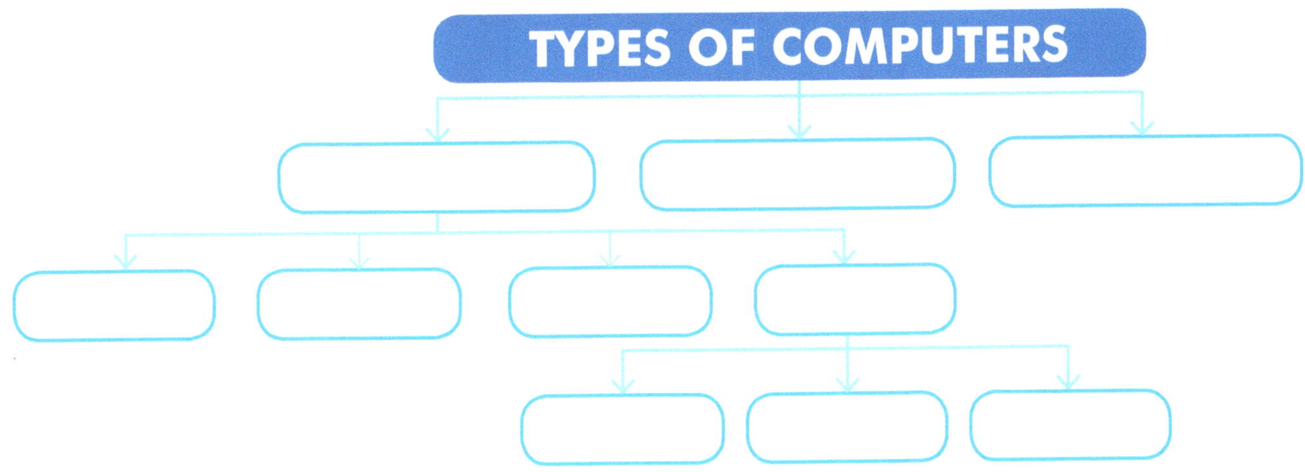

3. Identify the machines that use hybrid computers:

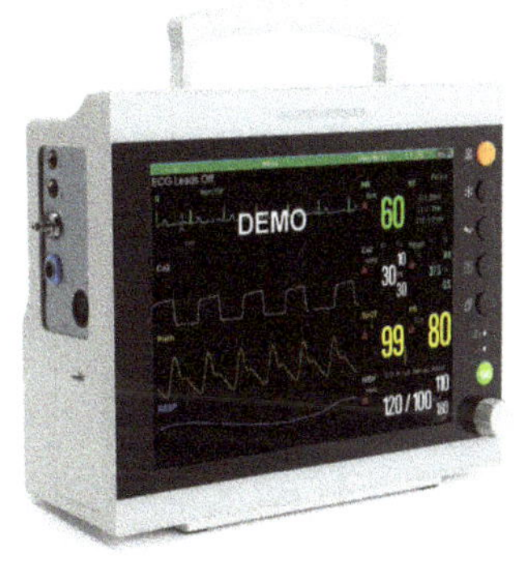

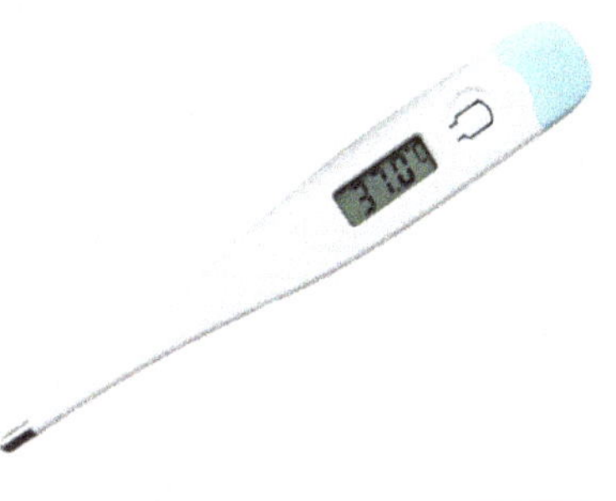

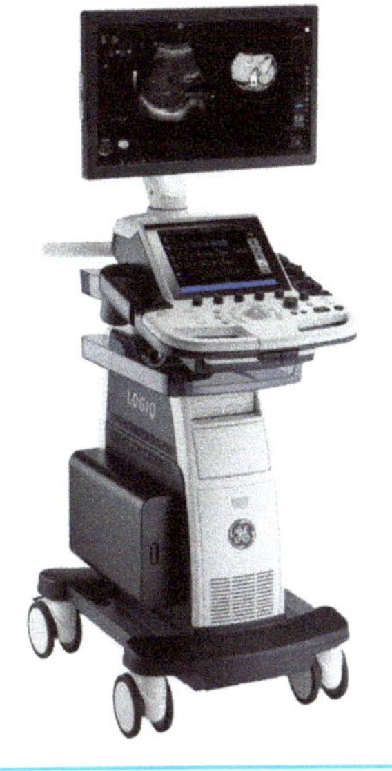

Characteristics and Applications of Computer

Dear children! After knowing the origin and types of computers let's move ahead and learn the capabilities of the computer. Nowadays computers have many uses and are used in every field of life. Today you will study the different characteristics and uses of the computer.

CHARACTERISTICS OF COMPUTER

Man developed computers so that it might perform complicated operations for him such as calculation and data processing or entertainment. Today, computers are everywhere — in our offices, homes, appliances and automobiles. The list is endless. The computer has become the integral part of our life and changed our life, mostly for the better. Let us discuss some of the characteristics of a computer, which make it an essential part of every emerging technology.

Computer

Fast Speed

The computer processes data at an extremely fast speed, *i.e.* millions or billions of instructions per second. In a few seconds, a computer can perform a huge task that a normal human being may take days or even years to complete. The speed of a computer is measured in megahertz (MHz), *i.e.* one million instructions per second.

Accuracy

Besides working at a very fast speed, computers are also very accurate. The level of accuracy depends on the instructions and the type of machines being used. Since we know that the computer is capable of doing only what it is instructed to do, wrong instructions for processing the data automatically lead to wrong results. The wrong results due to wrong instructions or incorrect input data are known as GIGO, i.e. garbage in, garbage out.

Storage Capacity

Computers can store large amounts of data. They can recall the required information almost immediately. The main memory of the computer is relatively small and it can hold only a certain amount of information. Therefore, the data is stored on secondary memory, such as hard disk or CD-ROM. The data from these devices can be accessed and brought into the main memory of the computer, as and when required, for processing.

Versatility

Computers can perform multiple tasks simultaneously with equal ease. For example, on the one hand it can be used to prepare a letter. On the other hand, it can be used to play music. In between one can print a document as well. All this work is possible by changing the program (sequence of instructions for computer).

Diligence

The computer being a machine does not get tired and lack concentration. If ten million calculations have to be performed, then the computer will perform the last ten-millionth calculation with the same accuracy and speed as the first calculation.

Sharing Resources

The computer in the past was a stand-alone device. But now computers have the capability to connect with one another. This has made the sharing of resources, data and information to a group of computers.

USES OF COMPUTER IN DIFFERENT FIELDS

Anywhere you go, whatever you do, you can see the amazing things that the computer has been doing for us. From the time we wake up, go to school or to our office, then back to our home for end-of-day activities, we make use of gadgets and machines powered by computers.

Communication

Computers make all modern communication possible. They operate telephone switching systems, coordinate satellite launches and operations, and control the equipment in all phases of television and radio broadcasts.

Transport

The computer helps in the working of the railway, airlines, shipping departments. The booking is done through computers and can also be checked through computers.

Science and Research

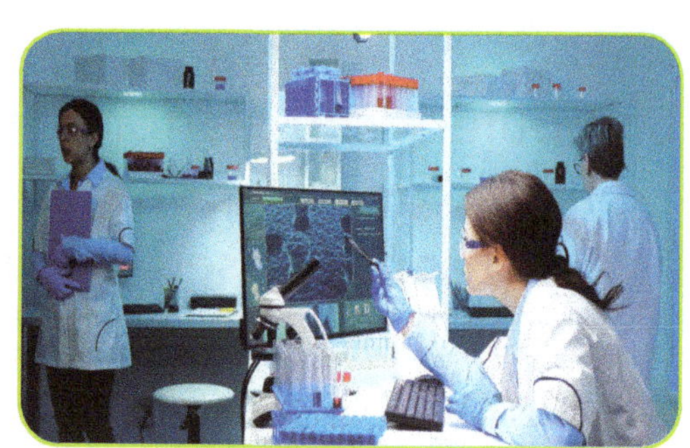

The computers are used by scientists and researchers in many ways to collect, store, manipulate and analyze data. Scientists can test new theories and designs on the computer. Computer-aided design or CAD programs enable engineers and architects to design three-dimensional models on a computer-screen. Flight simulators are valuable training tools for pilots.

Industry

Computers have opened a new era in manufacturing and consumer-product development. In the factory, computer-assisted manufacturing or CAM programs help people plan complex production schedules, keep track of inventories and accounts and control robots.

Government

Government agencies are the largest users of mainframes and supercomputers. They use computers for thousands of tasks, including research, breaking codes and interpreting data from satellites. The Inland Revenue uses computers to keep track of tens of millions of tax returns. Computers are also essential for taking the census, maintaining criminal records and many other tasks.

Education

Computers have become a valuable educational tool. Computer Assisted Instruction, or CAI, uses computerized lessons that range from simple practice sessions to complex interactive tutorials. These programmes have become essential teaching tools in medical and military training centres, where the topics are complex and the cost of human teachers is extremely high. Educational aids, such as encyclopaedias and reference works, are available to computer users.

Art and Entertainment

The constantly improving graphics and sound capabilities of personal computers have made them popular tools for many artists and musicians. Personal computers can display millions of colours and produce images clearly. Painting and drawing programmes enable artists to create realistic images and animated displays much more easily than they could with more traditional tools. The computer can get connected to various musical instruments and synthesizers. Musicians can use computers to create multiple-voice compositions and to play back music with hundreds of variations. Video games are one of the most popular applications of personal computers.

LIMITATIONS OF COMPUTER

A computer does many things. Actually, this is not the computer that performs various actions but it is the user since the computer is a man-made machine. Despite its various features, a computer does have the following limitations:

No Self-Intelligence

Today, a computer is able to do a piece of work which is impossible for man.

Computers are used to do risky and dangerous work and where actually sharp intellect is needed. But it does not have any intelligence of its own. It works according to the instructions given by users only.

No Decision-Making Power

The computer cannot take any decision of its own. It does only those tasks which are already instructed to it.

No Learning Power

The computer has no learning power. Once you give instructions to a computer how to perform a task, the very task is performed but it cannot perform again if you do not give it any instructions for the next time. For example, when you are taught how to solve a problem and if the same type of problem is given to you to solve, then you can do it because you have learnt to solve the problem.

Emotionless

Computers are emotionless. They do not have emotions, like love, hatred. They are simply machines which work as per the instructions given to them.

Restrict Human Capability

Although computers are great help to human beings yet it is commonly felt that we have become so dependent on them that we cannot make very simple calculations without them. Sometimes, we cannot speak out even those telephone numbers instantly which we use every now and then as we have got the habit of using them by retrieving the storage.

Health Problems

The excessive use of computers is causing various types of health problems such as cervical and back pain, pain in eyes, headache.

Privacy Problems

Nowadays we store all the important information, like medical records, credit reports, tax records and every life-event in a computer somewhere. Sometimes if the confidential records are not protected properly, users might find their privacy violated and identities stolen.

Public Safety

Many adults, teens and children around the world use computers to share their photos, videos, journals, music and other personal information. Sometimes these innocent people have fallen victim to crimes committed by dangerous strangers.

LET'S HAVE A LOOK

- Today computers are used everywhere - in offices, homes, appliances and automobiles.
- The computer processes data at a very fast speed.
- The speed of the computer is measured in megahertz (MHz).
- The computer can perform multiple tasks simultaneously.
- The computer can be used for communication, science and research, industry, a government agency, education, art and entertainment.
- Despite its various features, a computer does have some limitations as well.

BRAIN TEASER

1. Answer the following questions:

a. What are the characteristics of a computer? Explain any two of them.

____

____

b. What is the role of a computer in art and entertainment?

____

____

c. How is a computer helpful to a government agency?

____

____

d. Computers have opened a new era in manufacturing and in the development of consumer products. How?

____

____

e. What are the limitations of a computer? Explain any two of them.

____

____

2. Fill in the blanks:

a. The computer processes data at an ______________ fast speed.

b. The level of ______________ depends on instructions.

c. A computer can perform ______________ tasks simultaneously.

d. ______________ are valuable training tools for pilots.

e. ______________ uses computerized lessons in the field of education.

f. Musicians can use computers to create ______________ compositions.

3. Write '**T**' for true and '**F**' for false in the boxes:

a. The speed of a computer is measured in bits and bytes. ☐

b. You cannot store text and graphic files in computers. ☐

c. A computer can perform millions of operations in a second. ☐

d. A computer gets tired after working for long hours. ☐

e. You cannot communicate with the help of a computer. ☐

f. A computer has no learning power. ☐

4. Multiple Choice Questions

Tick (✓) the correct answer:

a. The speed of a computer is measured in

i. KB ☐ ii. MHz ☐ iii. KM ☐

b. The wrong results due to wrong instructions are known as

i. FIFO ☐ ii. CICO ☐ iii. GIGO ☐

c. The program used by engineers and architects for designing

i. CAD ☐ ii. CAM ☐ iii. CAI ☐

d. Government agencies are the largest users of mainframes and

i. Smartphones ☐ ii. Supercomputers ☐

iii. Laptops ☐

e. Excessive use of computers is causing various types of

i. Health problems ☐ ii. Accidents ☐

iii. Profits ☐

Visit a railway station, an airport, a mall, etc., and observe the working of computers there. Then write in your own words about them in MS-Word and save the file as 'Uses of Computers'.

Operating System - Windows 10

Dear students, you already know about Windows 10 as an operating system. Now let's move ahead and have some more knowledge and get more familiar with Windows 10.

OPERATING SYSTEM

As you all know, an operating system is a computer program that manages the resources of a computer. It accepts the inputs of a keyboard and a mouse from a user and displays the results of actions. It allows the user to run applications or communicate with other computers via network connections.

The computer consists of different parts and performs work at a time. It also requires a manager for it. The manager in a computer is called the Operating System.

An Operating System is an interface between the user and the computer system. An operating system is the first software you install in your computer that allows you to operate the computer.

Windows is an operating system developed by Microsoft Corporation.

Functions of Operating System

Operating system provides the basic rules according to which a computer should perform:

⇒ Starts and shuts down a computer
⇒ Manages programs
⇒ Coordinates tasks
⇒ Establishes an Internet connection
⇒ Provides utilities
⇒ Provides a user interface
⇒ Manages memory
⇒ Configures devices
⇒ Monitors performance
⇒ Controls a network

WINDOWS 10

Windows 10 is one of the most popular Operating Systems in the computer. It provides you with Graphical User Interface (GUI). GUI contains graphics icons and is commonly navigated by using a computer mouse. It is very user-friendly. Windows 10 was released on July 29, 2015.

Windows 10

Features of Windows 10

The interface of Windows 10 has very attractive and colourful themes. It comes with new features, improved programs and a faster speed. Among the new features available in Windows 10, there are new technologies that run in the background, making your computer more efficient and reliable.

It has security tools that are used to keep your computer more secure.

Windows 10 allows you to personalize your computer by changing your display settings, through the control panel of the computer.

It also helps to manage different resources and software functioning of the computer system.

Starting Windows 10

After TURNING ON the computer, the computer starts some processing. After some time, a Welcome Screen appears.

A password may be asked. After giving the password, a final screen appears. This final screen is called Desktop.

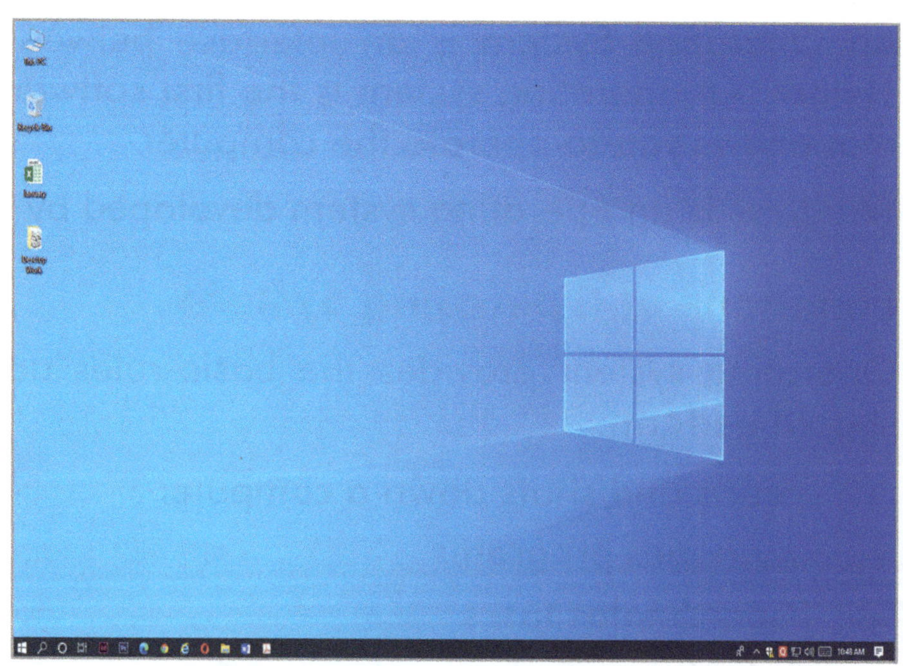

Windows Desktop

Windows 10 Screen

Windows 10 screen has different components, such as:

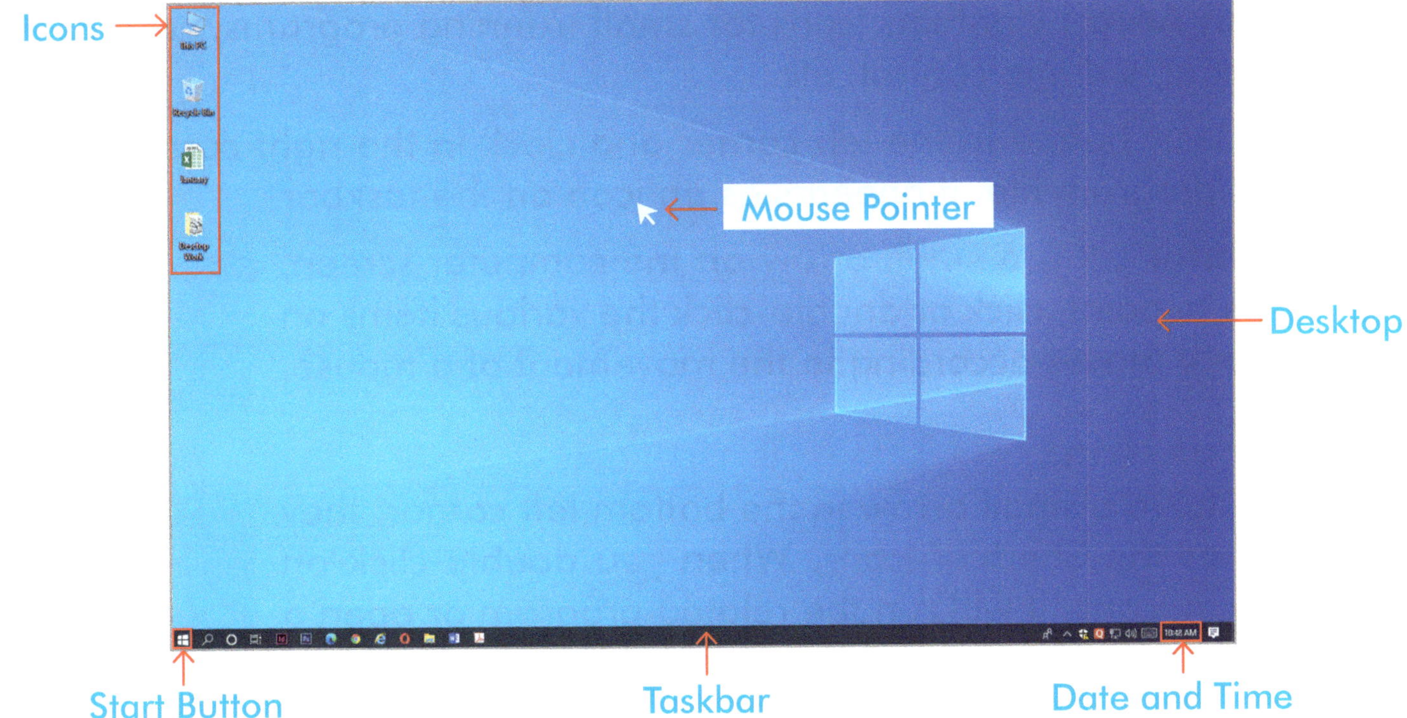

Desktop : The very first screen that appears after turning on the computer is called Desktop. It is large area that is the upper part of the computer screen, also known as the 'work area.' The major purpose of the desktop is to hold shortcut icons and other components that help you to work efficiently.

Icons : Icons on the desktop are the small pictures that represent objects or programs. You can open any icon by double-clicking on it with the mouse.

Task Bar : A row of icons at the bottom of the desktop is called Task Bar. The Windows 10 taskbar mainly has four main sections:

Start Button : Labelled with the Windows logo, it displays the Start menu.

Quick Launch : Allows certain applications to be accessed with a single click.

Running Programs : Allows easy access to all running programs.

Notification Area : Contains icons for small running programs, such as the clock, calendar, volume control, etc.

It contains Start button in the left corner and clock in the right corner. When you open a program file, it appears as an icon on the taskbar.

Mouse Pointer : It is a small arrow on the computer screen, which helps to point, click or double-click the various items on the desktop. It moves according to the movement of a mouse.

More about Icons

Some icons have a small arrow in the bottom left corner; they are known as the Shortcut Icons. When you double-click on these shortcut icons, it will run the related program or open a document accordingly.

This PC

This PC allows the user to access and see the local drives and external drives available in the computer.

Local drives : These drives display the hard disk (storage device) of your computer. When you double-click on this icon, a window appears to display the contents of the hard disk drive.

External drives (Removable Storage) - (DVD RW Drive) : These drives show the data in your CD-ROM or Pen drive you insert in your computer.

You can double-click on this icon to view the contents of the disk drive.

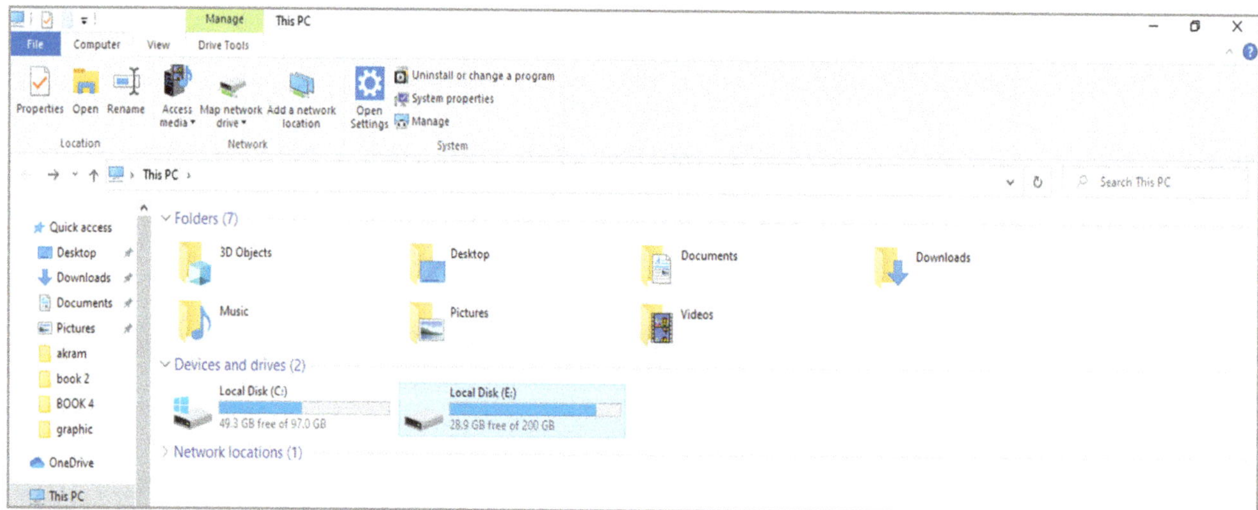

Recycle Bin : When you delete a file or folder in Windows Operating System, it is moved to the Recycle Bin. Even after you have deleted the files, you can always restore them from the Recycle Bin.

EXPLORING START MENU

The start menu is the main entrance to the programs folders and settings of your computer. It is called menu because it provides a list of choices, just as a restaurant menu does. As 'Start' implies, it is often the place that you will go to start or open things.

Opening Start Menu

To open the Start menu, click on the Start button in the lower-left corner of the screen or press the Windows logo key on your keyboard.

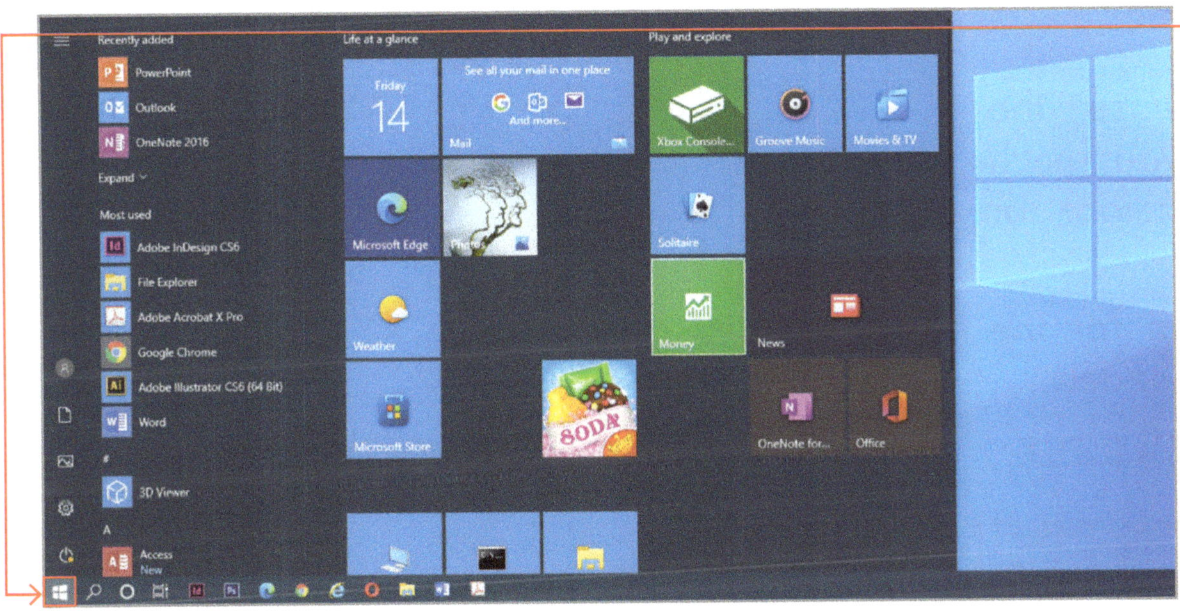

1. Click on Start button.

   The Start menu will appear.

The Start Menu has three parts:

The Menu, the All Apps list, and the Tiles area.

The Menu flushes up against the left edge and provides shortcuts to the settings, documents, and pictures. Here we can also Restart or Shut down the PC.

Next to the Menu is the All Apps list. At the top, you may see categories for **Recently Added, Most Used**, and Suggested categories followed by all apps and programs installed on your PC. Some of these are clearly listed while others will reside within parent folders. This list scrolls separately from the Tiles area located on the right.

Tiles area in Windows 10 displays information in the form of Live tiles that are useful at a glance without opening an app. For example, the News tile displays headlines while the Weather tile displays the forecast. You can rearrange, resize, and move these tiles to make them work better for you.

While you can't disable the Tile area, you can unpin Tiles from the Start Menu.

Resize the Start Menu

If you want to change the size of the Start Menu, follow these steps:

Step 1: Place the cursor over the top or right edge until it becomes two arrows.

Step 2: Click and hold the left mouse button.

Step 3: Drag the mouse up or right, depending on the edge.

Step 4: Release the button when you reach the desired height or width.

Step 5: Repeat for the other side as needed.

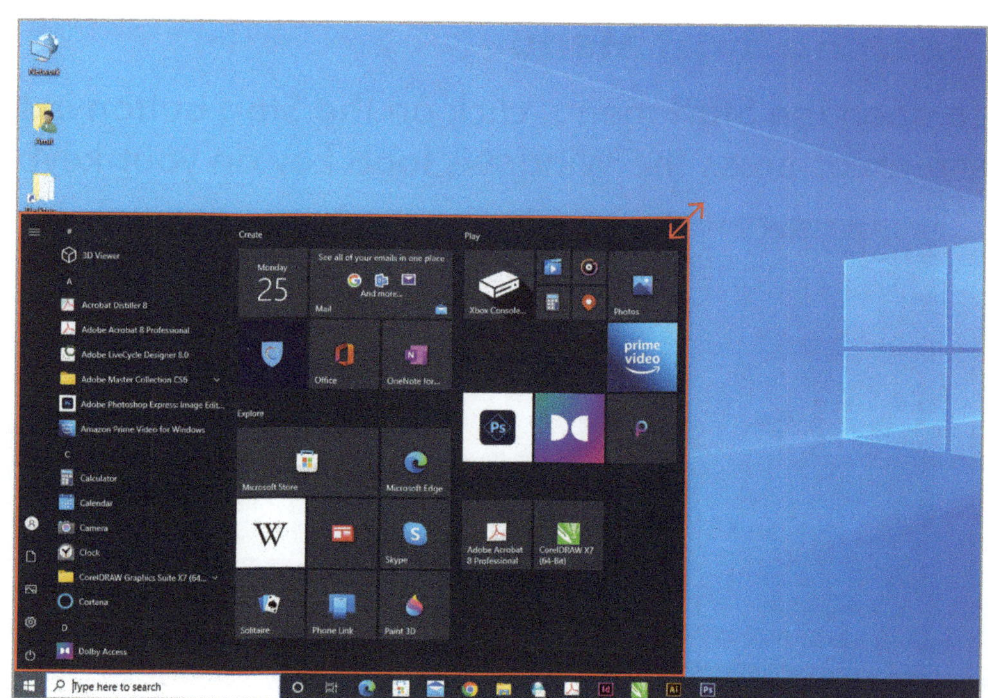

Note

You can place the cursor in the Start Menu's top-right corner and just drag that corner to resize both edges.

Making the menu larger vertically will give more space to the All Apps list and the Tiles area while adding horizontal space will only extend the Tiles. At its smallest horizontal setting, the Start Menu can only handle three medium columns of the smaller Tiles, but at its maximum setting, it can fit six.

Opening Program from the Start Menu

One of the most common uses of the Start menu is opening programs installed on your computer. To open a program, follow the steps as:

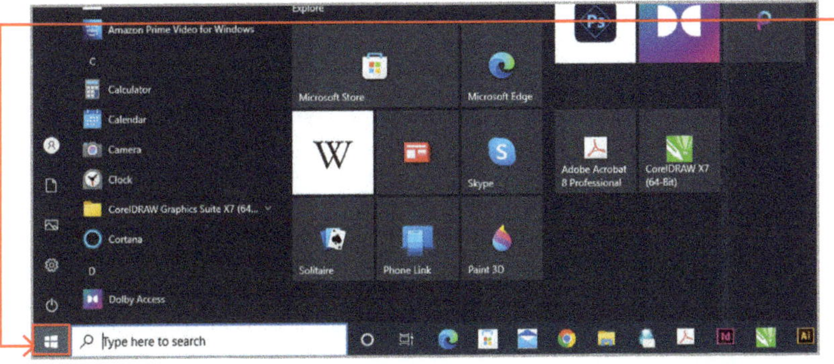

1. Click on Start button.

2. A list of All apps appears.

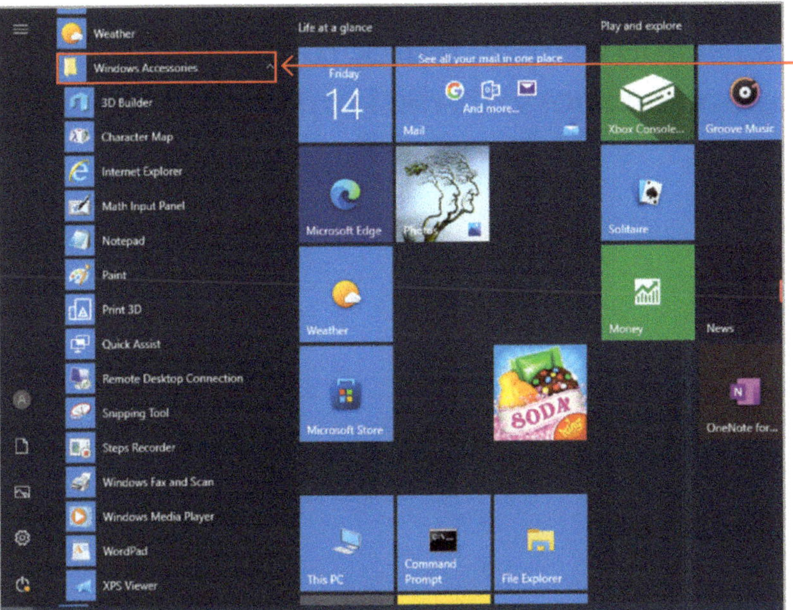

You can go to All apps and scroll down the app list to see all apps and programs alphabetically, from A to X.

3. Click on the Program you want to open.

Some programs have sub-menus.

In this example we choose Windows Accessories.

Windows Accessories sub-menu will appear.

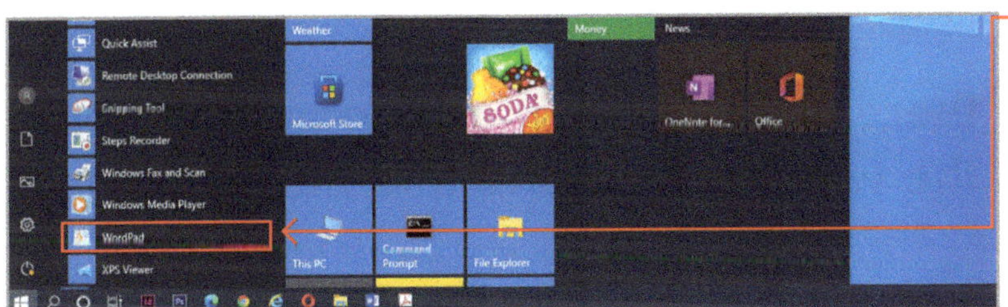

4. Click on WordPad from Windows Accessories sub-menu.

The WordPad window will appear.

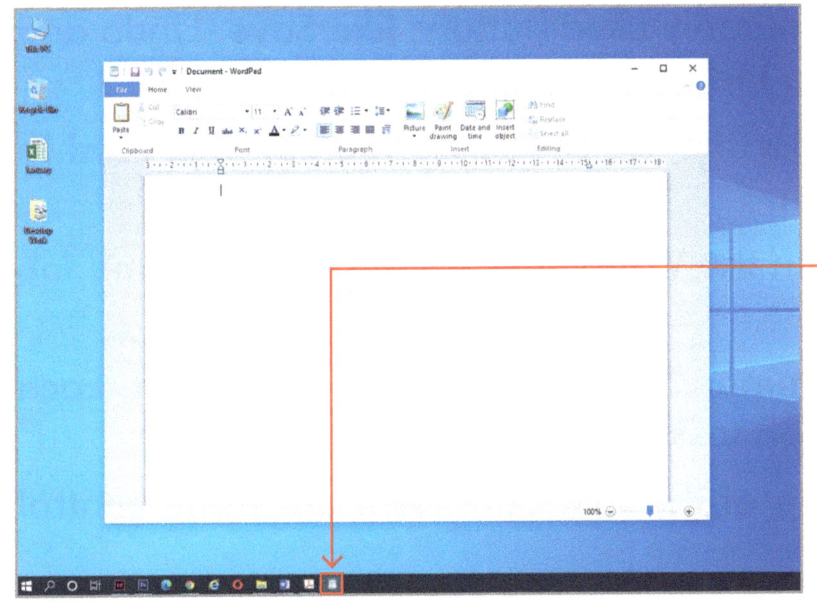

Windows 10 adds an icon for the program to the taskbar.

Do you know ?

In Windows 10, We can open a program by just typing the name of the program in the Search Box located on the Task Bar.

Typing triggers a search for what is being typed. Double-click on the program from the shown options to open it.

PROGRAM WINDOW

After using the steps from the previous section to open a program, a rectangular area surrounded by a frame and title bar appears on desktop. This is called a program window.

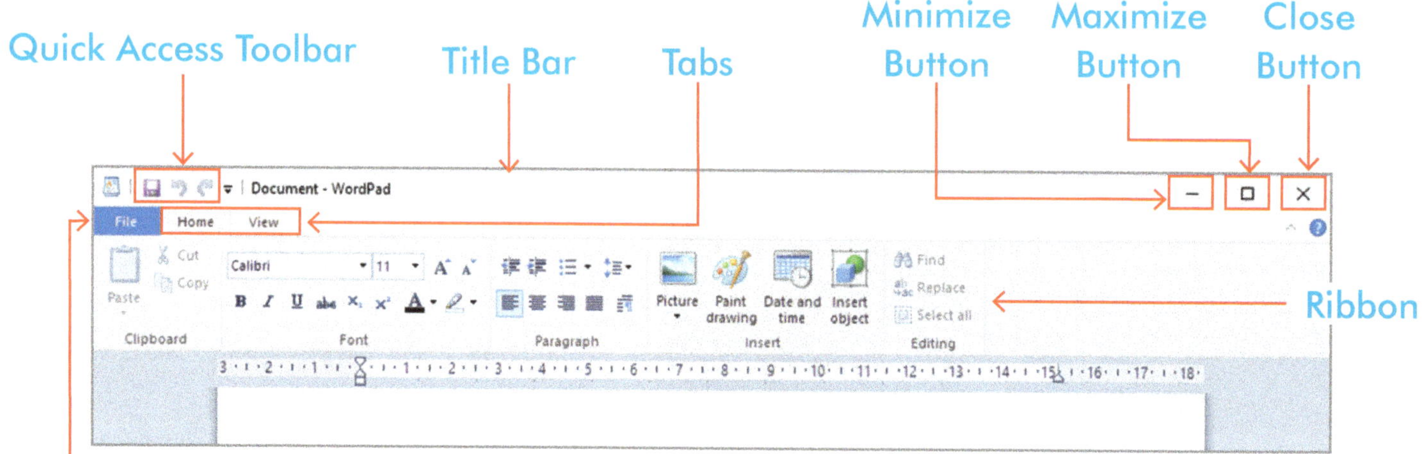

Title bar : At the top of the window there is a title bar that displays the name of the program. You can also move the window from the title bar by using a mouse.

Quick Access toolbar : On the left corner of the title bar there is a Quick Access Toolbar that contains the commonly used buttons like Save, Undo and Redo. More buttons can be added to the Quick Access Toolbar.

Program button : It is located under the Quick Access Toolbar. It is used to open the main menu of the program.

Tabs: There are two tabs available in the WordPad program — the Home tab and the View tab.

Ribbon : The groups of related commands in tabs are displayed on it. Each tab offers shortcut buttons to common tasks.

Control buttons : On the right side of the title bar, there are three control buttons.

⇒ **Maximize button –** This button is used to enlarge the size of the window to its maximum size, *i.e.* up to the entire desktop.

⇒ **Minimize button –** This button is used to display the window in its mininum size, *i.e.* on a taskbar as a windows taskbar icon.

⇒ **Close button –** This is used to close the window completely.

Maximizing a Window

With the help of maximize button, you can enlarge a window to its maximum size. To maximize the window:

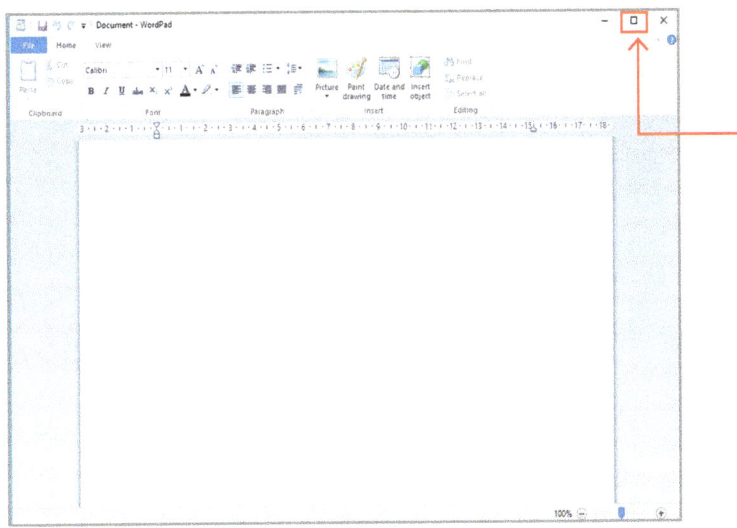

1. Click on Maximize button in the window.

   The window fills your entire desktop screen.

Minimizing a Window

With the help of minimize button, you can minimize the window to remove it from your screen if you are not using that window.

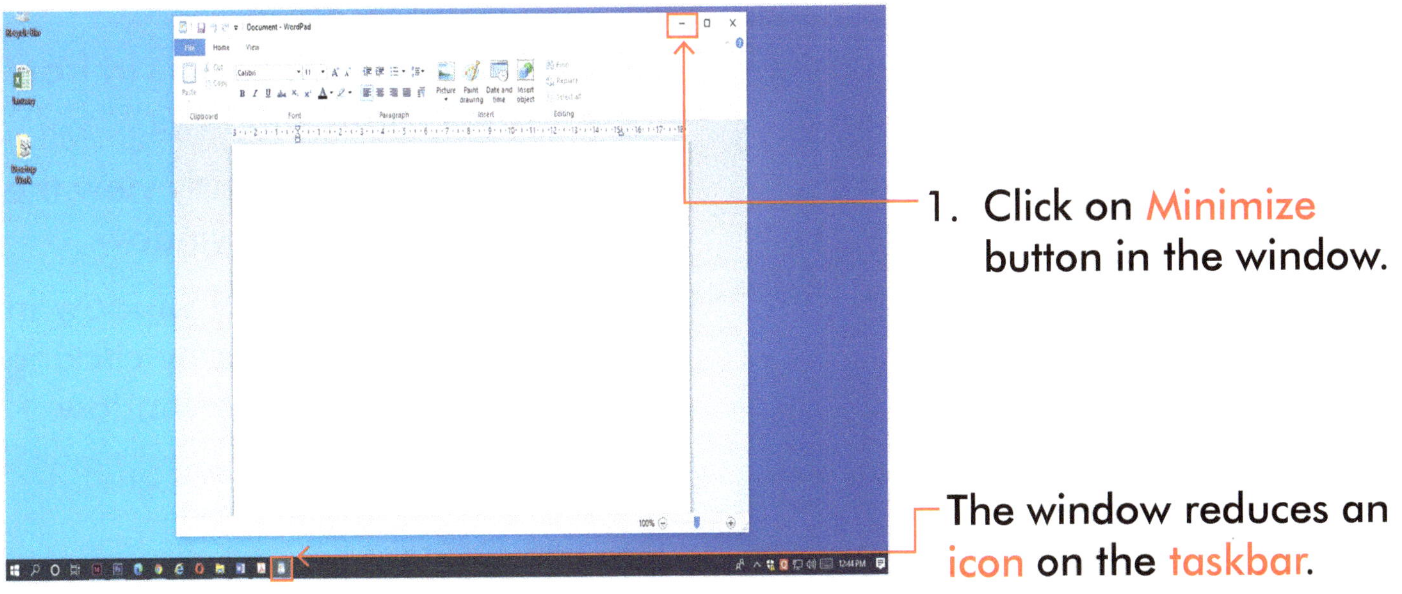

1. Click on Minimize button in the window.

The window reduces an icon on the taskbar.

You can re-display the window any time by clicking its icon on the taskbar.

Switching Between Windows

If you have opened more than one window, you can easily switch between them. By using the taskbar, you can switch between one program and another.

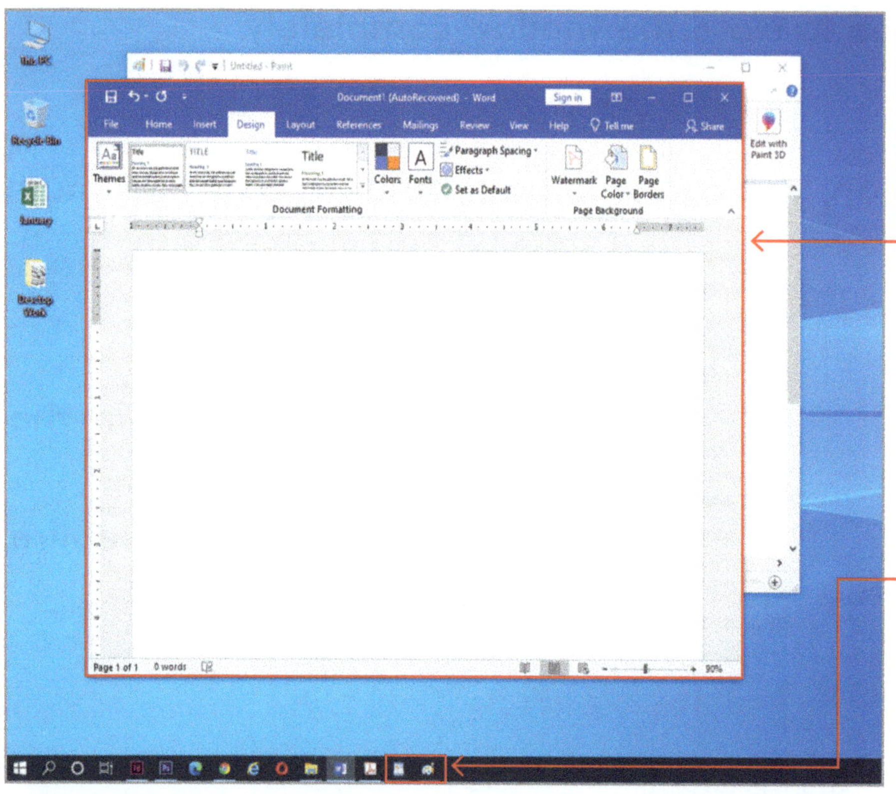

You can work only with one window at a time which is called the active window.

The active window appears in front of all other windows and displays a dark title bar.

The taskbar displays an icon for each open window on your screen.

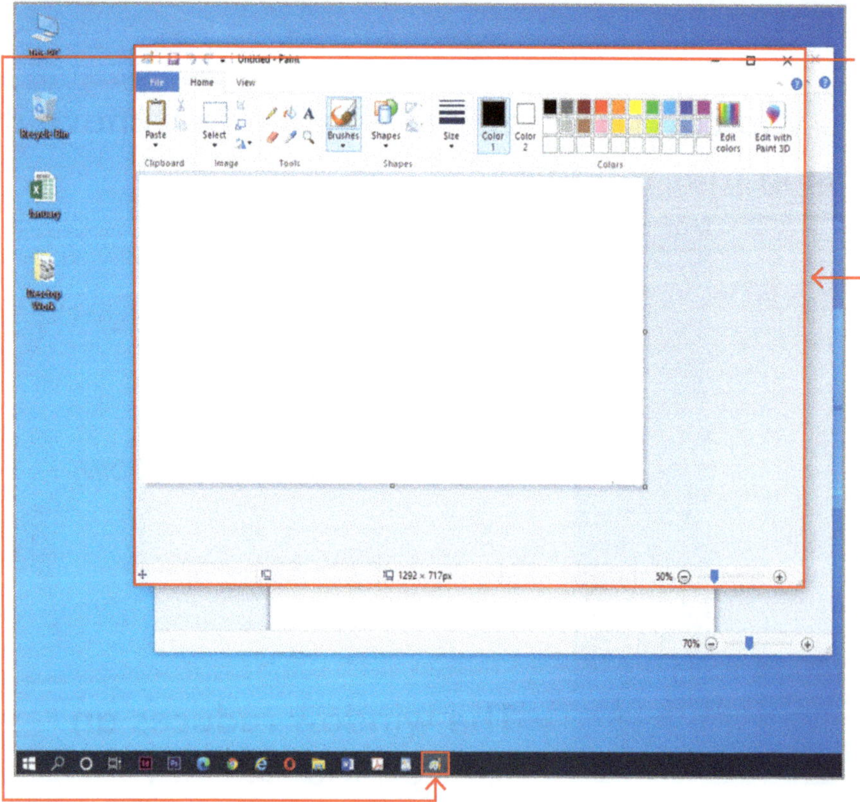

1. To display the window you want to work in front of all other windows, click its icon on the taskbar.

   The window appears in front of all other windows.

   You can now clearly view the contents of the window.

You can also display window in front of all windows by clicking anywhere inside the window.

Showing Desktop Using Aero Peek

Aero peek or Show Desktop is a button on the far right corner of the taskbar It is used to minimize your entire screen instantly to view the desktop clearly.

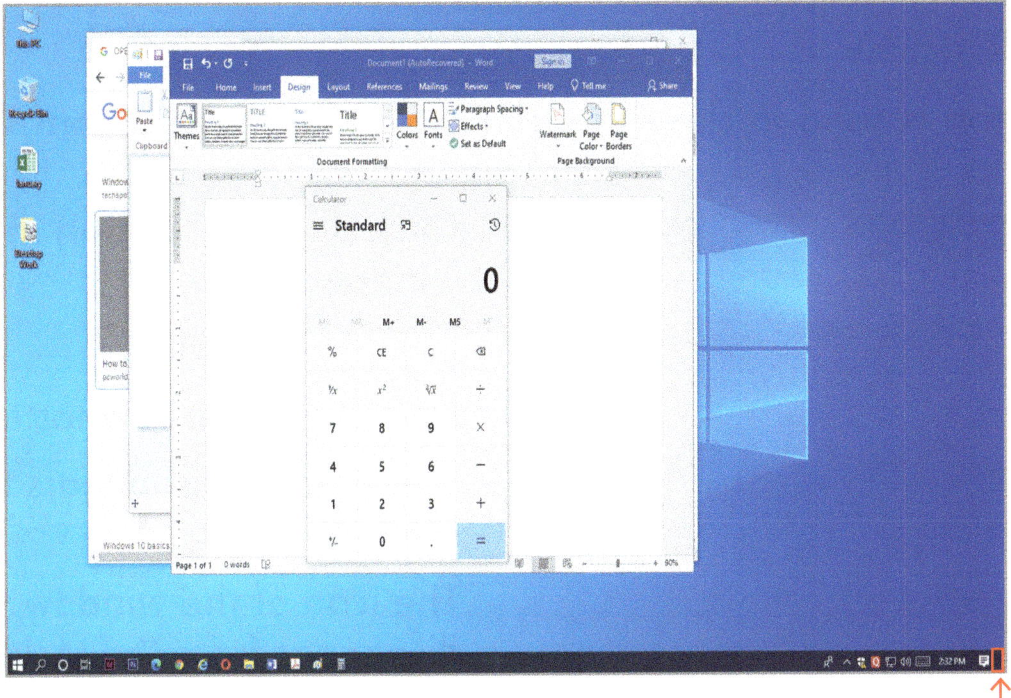

1. Move your mouse pointer on the Show Desktop button towards the far right corner of the taskbar.

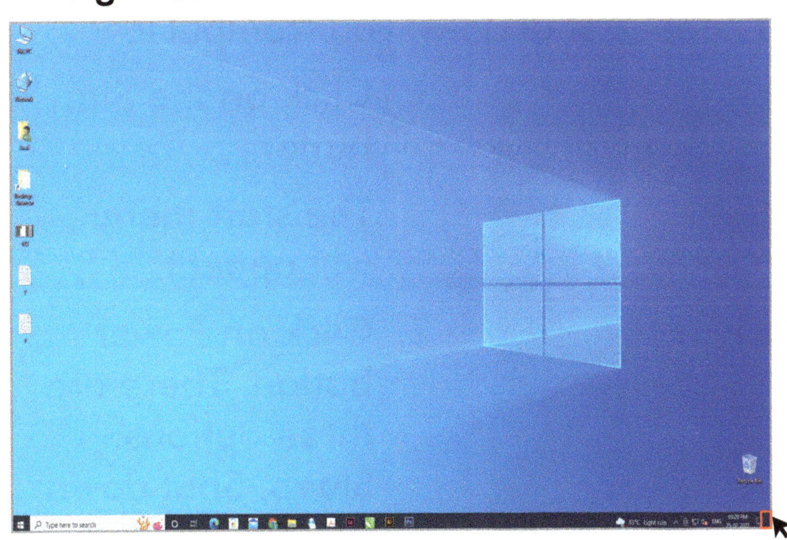

When you take the mouse pointer on the Show Desktop button, all the windows become transparent.

You can see the desktop.

2. To view the desktop clearly, click on the Show Desktop button.

   Each window minimizes an icon on the taskbar. You can now clearly view the desktop.

   If you want to redisplay all windows, click again on Show Desktop button.

   To display only one window, click its icon on the taskbar.

Do you know ?

You can fix two windows together on the screen by pressing Windows button and left arrow key for one window and Windows button and right arrow key for the other window.

Closing a Window

The Close button is used to close the window and remove it from the desktop screen.

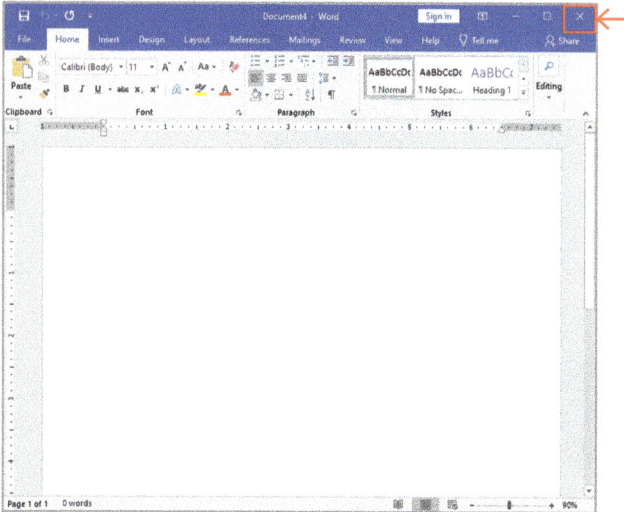

1. Click on Close button in the window.

Or

Press Alt+F4 as a shortcut key.

The window disappears from your screen.

The icon of the window will disappear from the taskbar.

Shutting Down Windows 10

Once you have finished your work, you need to shut down your computer.

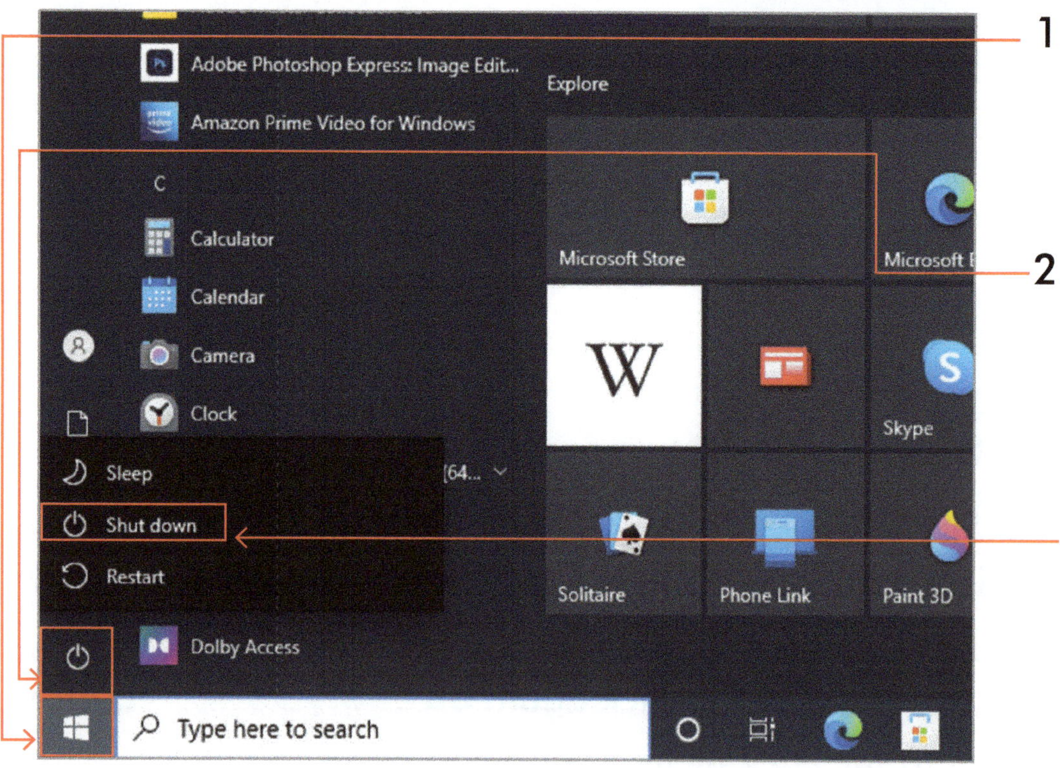

1. Click on the Start button.

   The start menu will appear.

2. Click on Power button. There are three options: Sleep, Shut down, Restart.

   Click on the Shut Down button.

   Windows shuts down and Turns Off the computer.

LET'S HAVE A LOOK

- An operating system is a computer program that manages the resources of a computer.
- Windows 10 screen contains various components such as Desktop, Icons, Taskbar, Start button, Mouse pointer, Quick Launch toolbar and Notification area.
- The Start menu is the main entrance to the programs, folders and settings in a computer.
- The most common use of the Start menu is opening programs installed in your computer.
- The search box is one of the convenient ways to find things on a computer.
- The right pane of the Start menu contains links to the parts of Windows that you are likely to use frequently.
- A program window is a rectangular area on the desktop surrounded by a frame and title bar at the top.

BRAIN TEASER

1. Answer the following questions:

a. What is the use of an operating system?

____

____

b. What are the various functions of an operating system?

____

____

c. What is GUI?

____

____

d. Give a brief note on the features of Windows 10.

____

____

e. What is the use of icons on a desktop?

____

____

f. What is start menu used for and why is it called so?

g. What are the three basic parts of the Start Menu?

h. What is the use of search box?

2. Answer each of the following in one word or line:

a. Name the most popular operating system.

b. Write the full form of GUI.

c. Name the most common function of Windows 10.

d. Name the different components of Windows 10 screen.

e. Name the three basic parts of Start menu.

3. Define the following:

a. Desktop

b. Icons

c. Start button

d. Mouse Pointer

e. Taskbar

4. Multiple Choice Questions

Tick (✓) the correct answer:

a. Microsoft Windows provides you with

i. GUI ☐ ii. PUI ☐ iii. Commands ☐

b. The small pictorial symbols on desktop are

i. Programs ☐ ii. Icons ☐ iii. Pointers ☐

c. The area where clock is shown

i. Notification ☐ ii. Start button ☐ iii. Icons ☐

d. Icons that have a small arrow at the bottom left corner are called

i. Taskbar ☐ ii. Shortcut Icons ☐ iii. Folders ☐

e. It opens window where you can access disk drives

i. Music ☐ ii. This-PC ☐ iii. Document ☐

5. Write 'T' for true and 'F' for false in the boxes:

a. Windows 10 is an operating system developed by IBM. ☐

b. Starting or restarting a computer is a function of the computer. ☐

c. Desktop is the first screen that appears after Switching On the computer. ☐

d. The Title bar is located at the bottom of the window. [ ]

e. You can open Start menu through Aero Peek. [ ]

f. The search box is used to find things on a computer. [ ]

g. Aero Peek button is located on the left side of the task bar. [ ]

6. Match the following:

a. Icons	i. The new feature in Windows 10
b. Clock	ii. The topmost bar on the window
c. Mouse pointer	iii. keyboard key used to open Start menu
d. Windows Key	iv. The small pictures on the desktop
e. Ribbon	v. A small arrow on the desktop
f. Title bar	vi. It displays the group of commands
g. Aero peek	vii. Shows the current time

ACTIVITY TIME

- **Learn the procedure to Turn On and Turn Off the computer.**
- **Explore the Start menu and make a list of the programs the menu contains.**
- **Try to resize the tiles you see on your start menu.**
- **Open and explore the program window.**

Formative Assessment-2
(Chapters 3-4)

1. Label the following:

a.

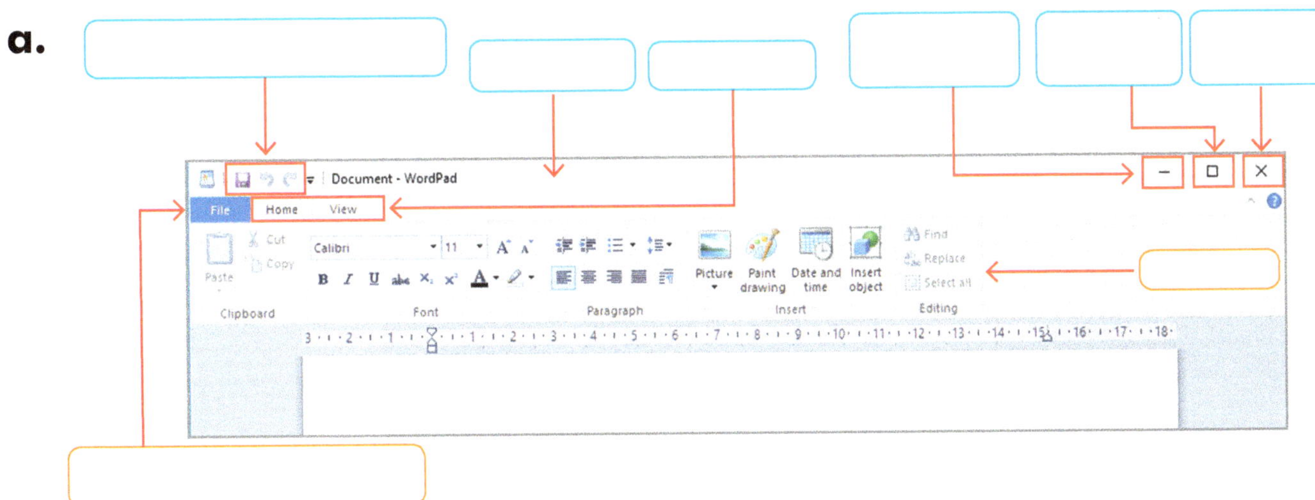

2. Label the following:

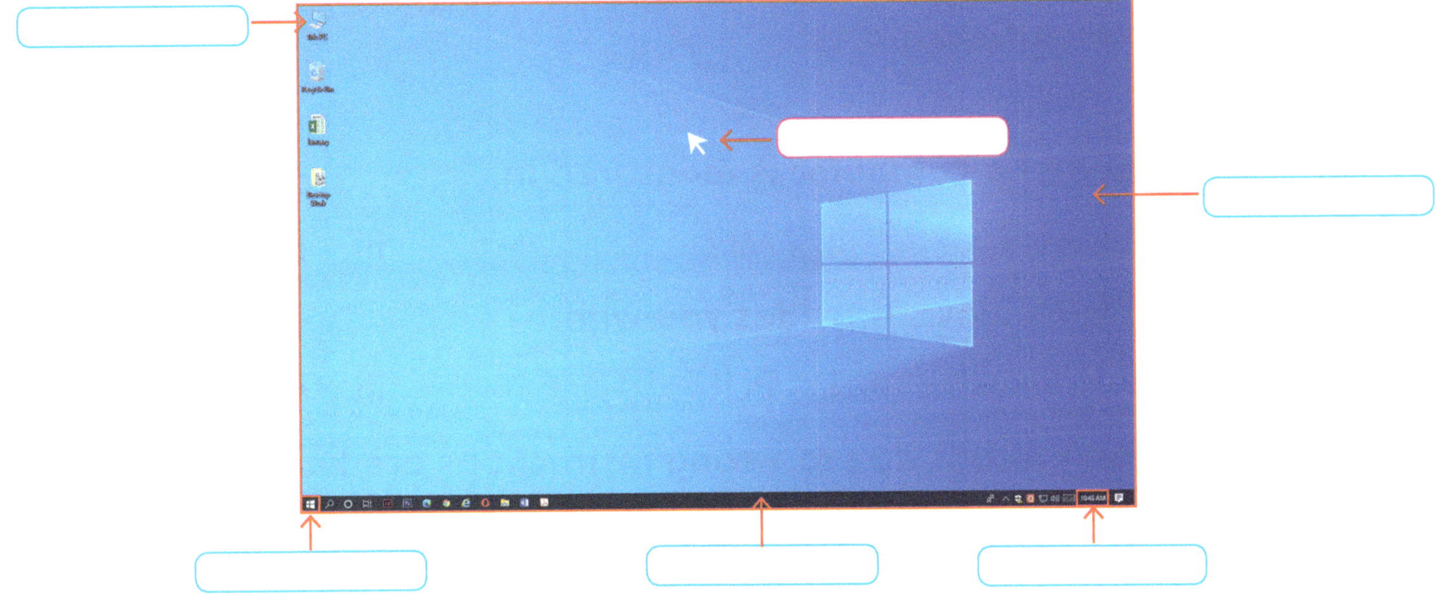

3. Write the names of the following icons.

4. Write steps to be followed to shut down Window 10. Also label the steps.

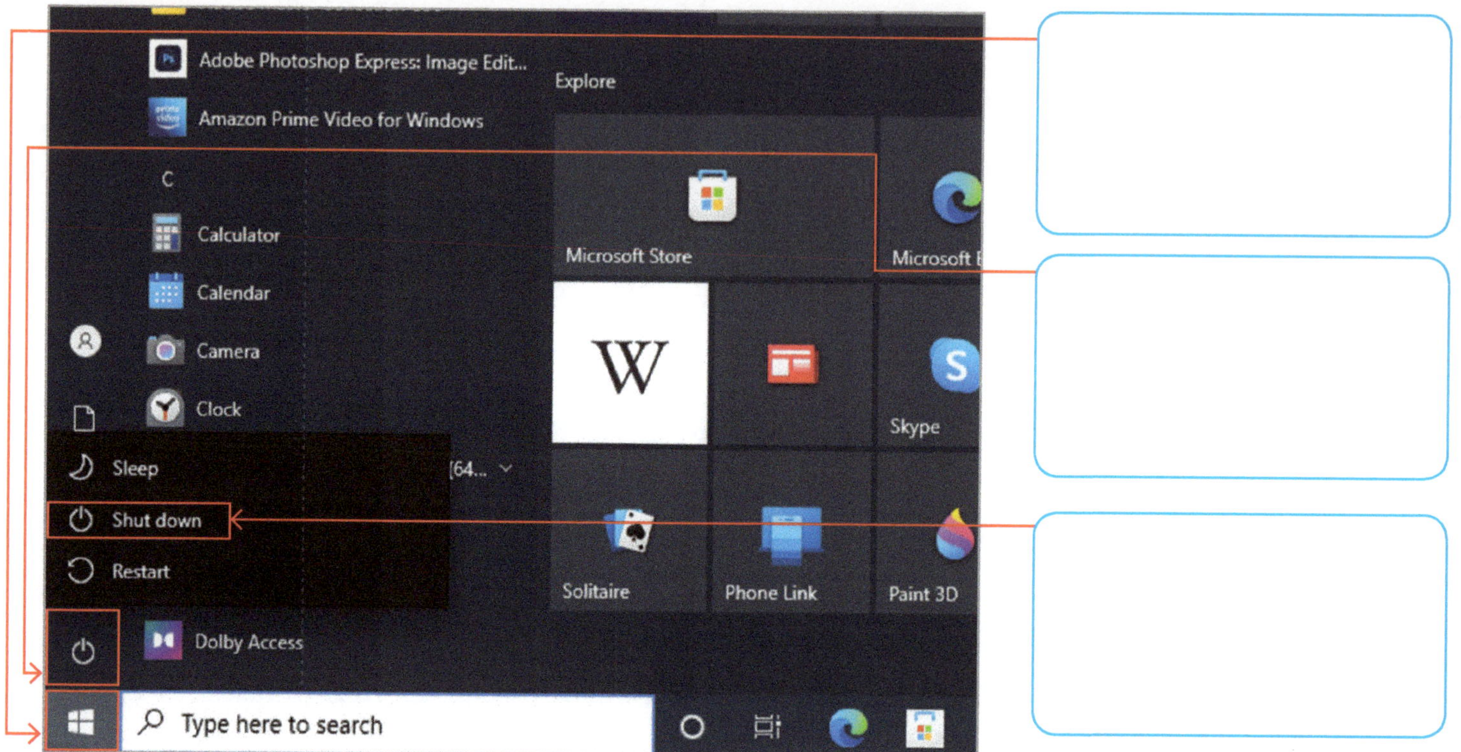

5. Multiple Choice Questions

Tick (✓) the correct answer:

a. The speed of a computer is measured in

i. KB ☐ ii. MHz ☐ iii. KM ☐

b. Microsoft Windows provides you with

i. GUI ☐ ii. PUI ☐ iii. Commands ☐

c. The wrong results due to wrong instructions are known as

i. FIFO ☐ ii. CICO ☐ iii. GIGO ☐

d. The small pictorial symbols on desktop are

i. Programs ☐ ii. Icons ☐ iii. Pointers ☐

e. The area where clock is shown

i. Notification ☐ ii. Start button ☐ iii. Icons ☐

f. The program used by engineers and architects for designing

i. CAD ☐ ii. CAM ☐ iii. CAI ☐

Summative Assessment-1
(Chapters 1-4)

1. Fill in the blanks:

a. The small arrow on the desktop is called ____________.

b. ____________ opens a window where you can access disk drives and other hardware connected to your computer.

c. The computer cannot take ____________ of its own.

d. ____________ are the biggest and powerful computers.

e. The computer was a combination of ____________ and ____________ of people, from across the world.

f. Blaise Pascal invented the Pascaline in ____________.

g. ____________ is also known as the father of computers.

h. PC-AT was introduced by ____________ in 1984.

i. ____________ computers are also called workstations.

j. The speed of a computer is measured in ____________.

2. Write 'T' for true and 'F' for false in the boxes:

a. UNIVAC was developed by John Presper Eckert. ☐

b. Micro computers are used for weather forecasting. ☐

c. Abacus was the first calculating device. ☐

d. Start button has five basic parts. ☐

e. The speed of the computer is measured in KM. ☐

f. The computer gets tired after doing work for long hours. ☐

g. Windows 10 is a GUI-based operating system. ☐

3. Answer the following:

a. Differentiate between a Micro computer and a Mainframe computer.

b. What are the limitations of the computer?

c. Write any four characteristics of the computer.

d. Write a short note on Charles Babbage.

e. Explain the three basic parts of Start menu.

f. How did earlier people do counting and record information?

g. What was the dream of Charles Babbage?

h. Explain Mark-I.

i. What is the processing speed of a Mainframe computer?

j. Differentiate between a laptop and a palmtop.

k. What is a hybrid computer?

l. What are the uses of the computer in education?

4. Match the following:

a.	Super computer	i.	John P. Eckert and J. Mauchly
b.	Mini computer	ii.	box-shaped
c.	PC-AT	iii.	Micro computer
d.	UNIVAC	iv.	button at the right corner
e.	Palmtop	v.	small pictures on desktop
f.	Start button	vi.	fastest computer ever made
g.	Aeropeek	vii.	IBM
h.	Icons	viii.	workstation

5 Personalizing Windows 10

Hello friends! You are familiar with Windows 10 screen. Now you can personalize the desktop of your computer by decorating it according to your choice and by changing background wallpaper and themes. Let us proceed.

CUSTOMISING THE DESKTOP

Customising the desktop means changing the desktop background and screen saver, applying a theme, etc.

Changing Desktop Background

Windows 10 lets us choose multiple background images for the desktop screen.

These background images are known as the desktop background or wallpaper. To change the wallpaper, follow these steps.

1. Right-click anywhere on the desktop and click on the Personalize option from the shortcut menu that appears

   The Settings window appears.

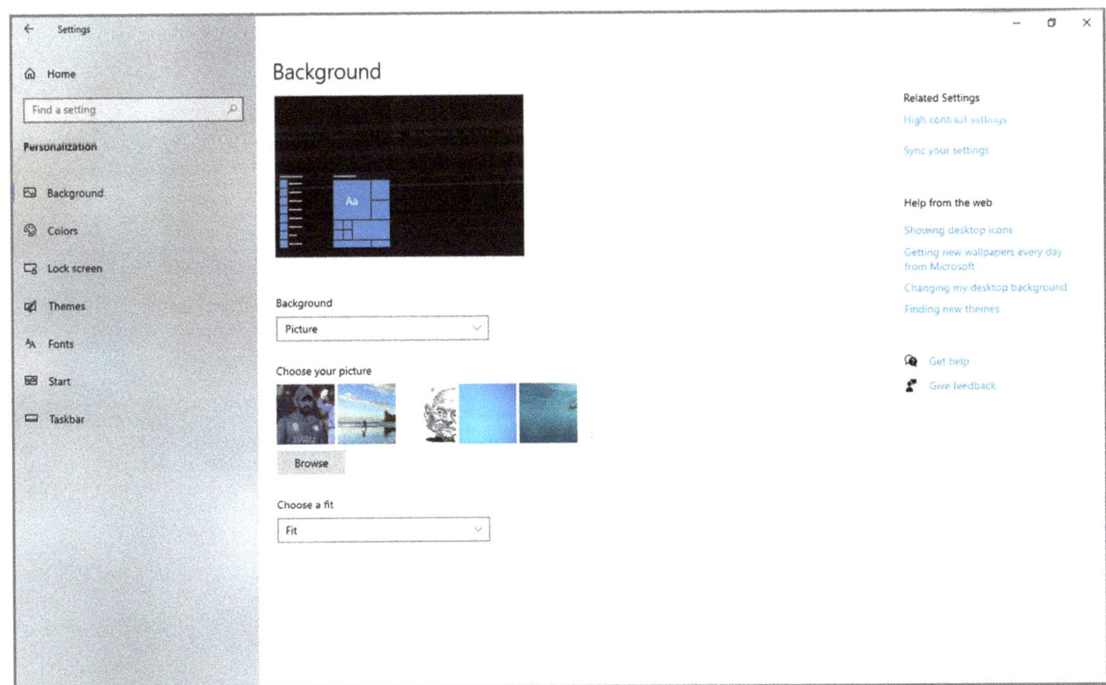

2. Click the drop-down arrow of the Background list box and select any option (Picture, Solid colour or Sideshow) from the list that appears. Let's select the Picture option.
3. Select any picture from the Choose your picture section.
4. Click the Close button (×) to close the Settings window. The selected picture is selected as the new desktop background.

CHANGING DESKTOP BACKGROUND

You can change the background of the desktop by applying different wallpapers to it.

Windows 10 provides you with a number of wallpapers. You can even download different wallpapers from the Internet.

1. Open the Personalization window.

Note

To open Personalization window, use the steps 1 to 3 from the previous section.

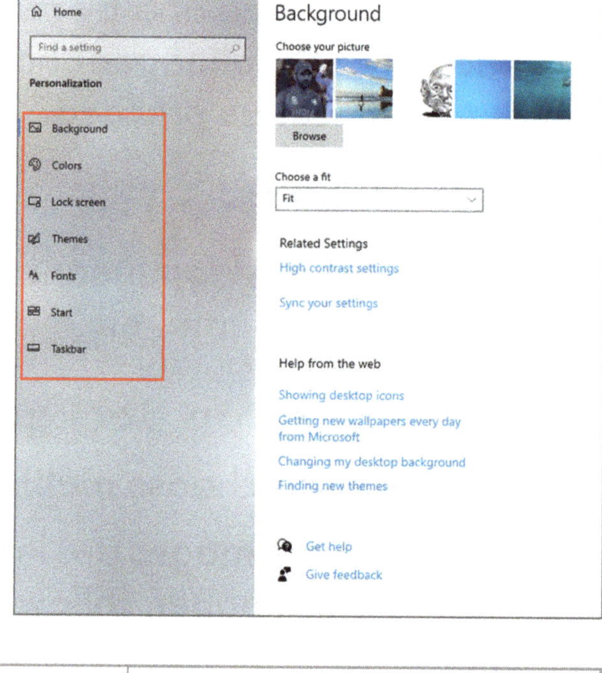

2. Click on Background.

   The Background window will appear.

3. Select the image you want to display.

   If you want to select your own images, click Browse and then use the Browse dialog box to select the file. Click Choose picture.

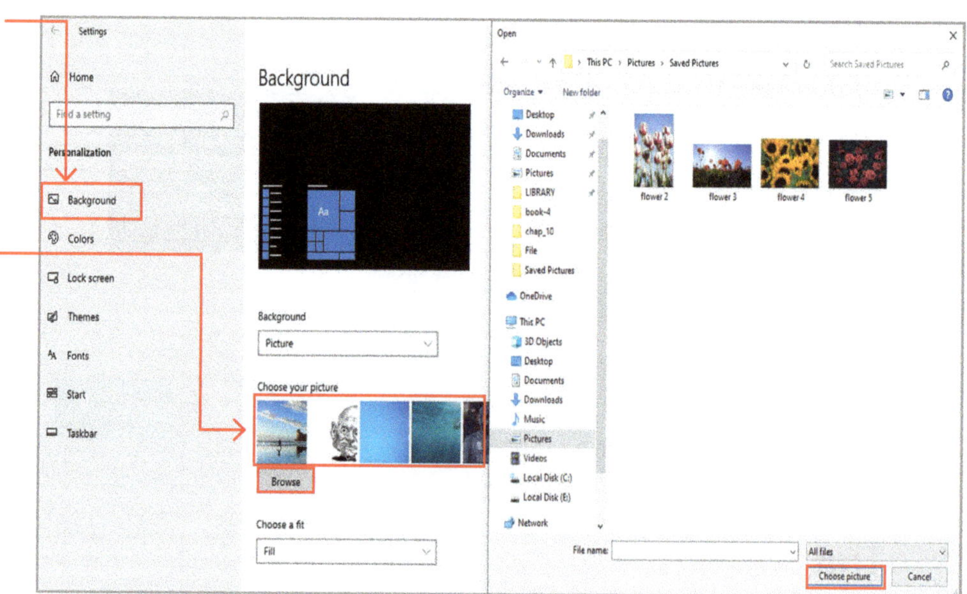

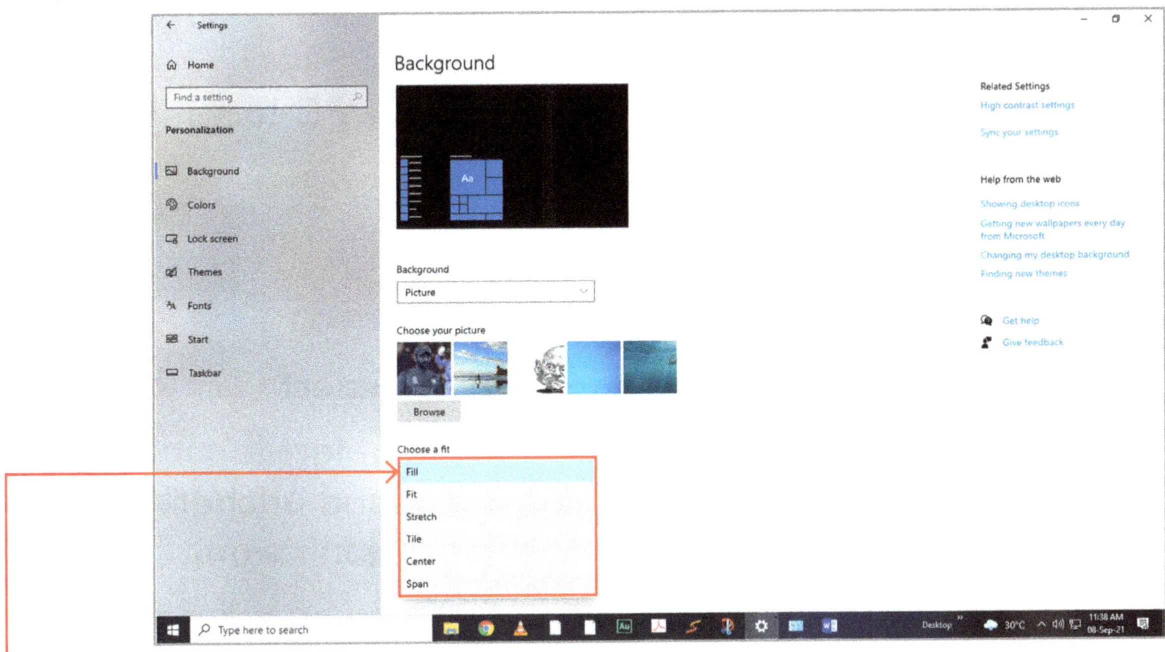

*** Picture Position (Step 7)**

Fill : This option displays a single copy of the image extended on all sides and keeps the ratio of width to height the same, so it means that some part of the image will cut off.

Fit : This option displays a single copy of the image extended until either the width of the picture fits the width of the screen or the height of the picture fits the height of the screen.

Stretch : This option displays a single copy of the image extended on all sides, so it fills the entire desktop.

Tile : This option displays multiple copies of the image repeated, so they fill the entire desktop.

Center : This option displays a single copy of the image in the centre of the screen.

The picture you selected appears on the desktop.

CUSTOMIZING LOCK SCREEN

Lock screen is the screen that appears when your PC locks itself after being unused for a while.

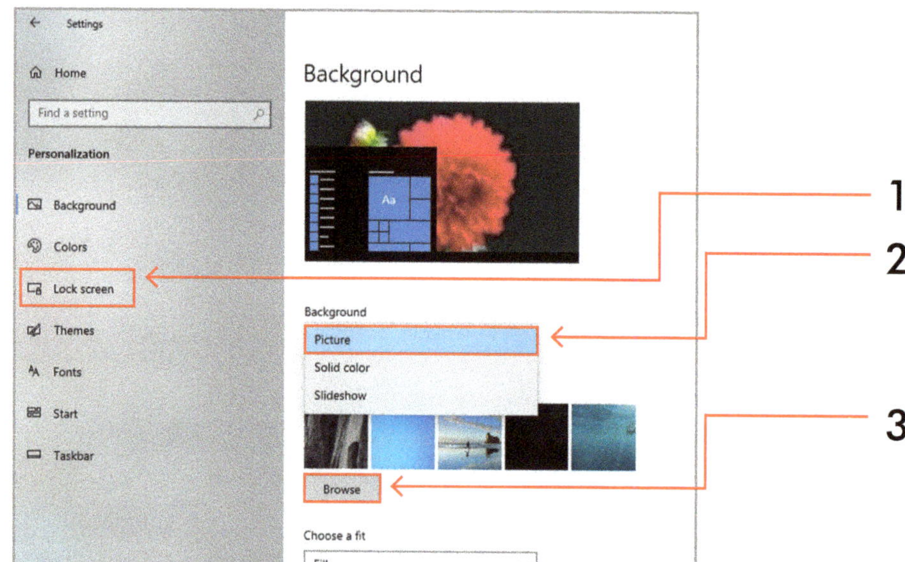

1. Select Lock screen.
2. Select the image you want and uncheck the image you don't want.
3. If you want to select your own image, click Browse.

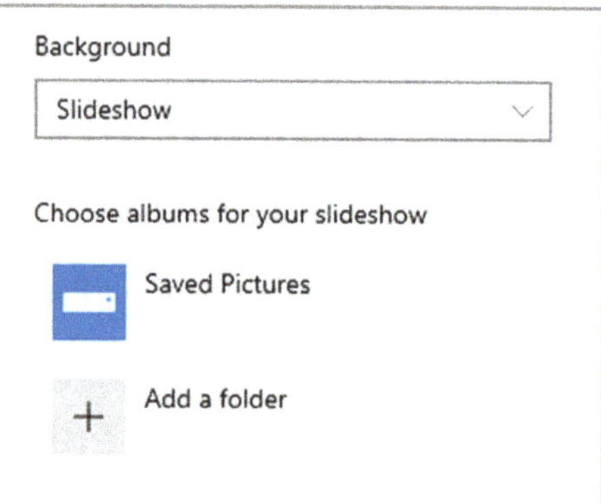

If you change the option here, Picture to Slideshow, you will get the option to choose multiple pictures for slideshow during Lock screen.

SETTING THE SCREEN SAVER

A screen saver is an animated image which is activated when your computer is not being used for a particular period of time. To come back again to the current screen, you just simply have to click the mouse or press any of the keys from the keyboard. To set the screen saver, follow the steps:

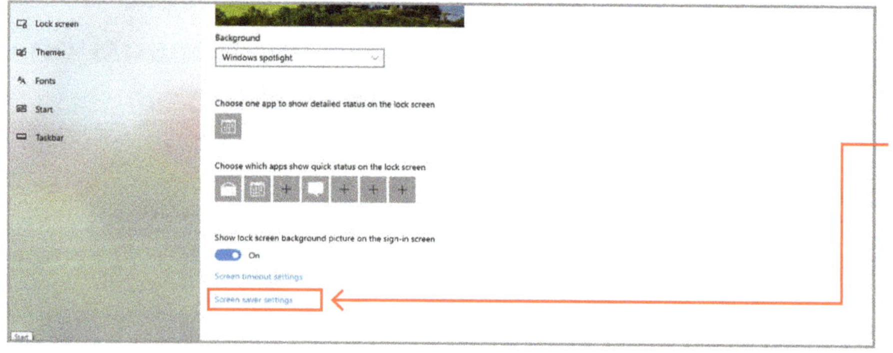

1. Open the Personalization window.
2. Click on Lock Screen and then select Screen Saver Settings.

   The Screen Saver Settings dialog box appears.

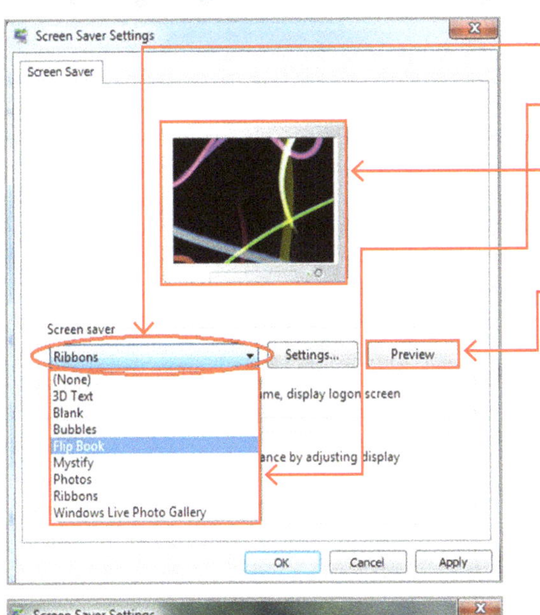

3. Click on the down arrow of Screen saver.
4. Click on the screen saver you want to use.

A preview of the screen saver appears.

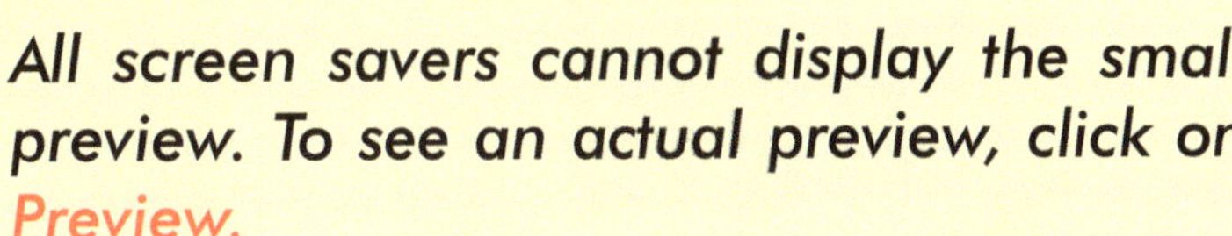

Note

All screen savers cannot display the small preview. To see an actual preview, click on Preview.

After this, move the mouse pointer or press a key to stop the preview.

5. Click on the Wait up and down arrow buttons to specify the number of minutes of idle time of the computer after which the screen saver will appear.
6. Click on OK.

The screen saver appears after your computer has been idle for the number of minutes you specified in Step 5.

Just move your mouse or press any key from the keyboard to bring back your Desktop again.

CHANGING THE COLOUR SCHEME

To make your computer colourful, you can choose different colour schemes provided in Windows 10. The colour scheme is applied to the window borders, taskbar and start menu. Follow the steps to change colour:

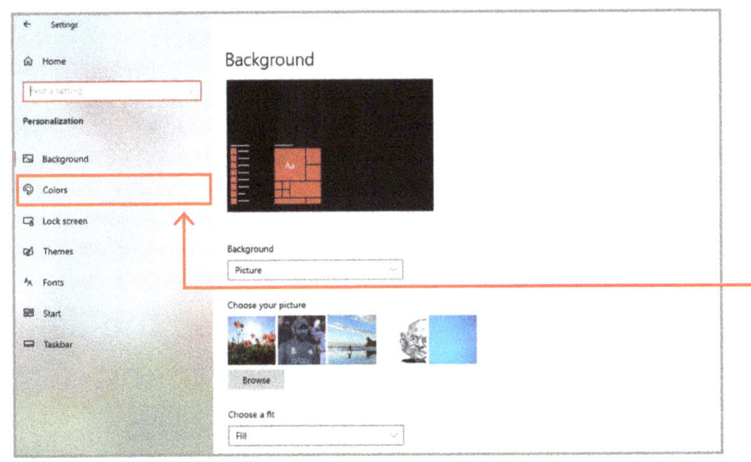

1. Open the Personalization window.
2. Click on Colors.
3. Scroll window using mouse and go to Choose your accent color section.

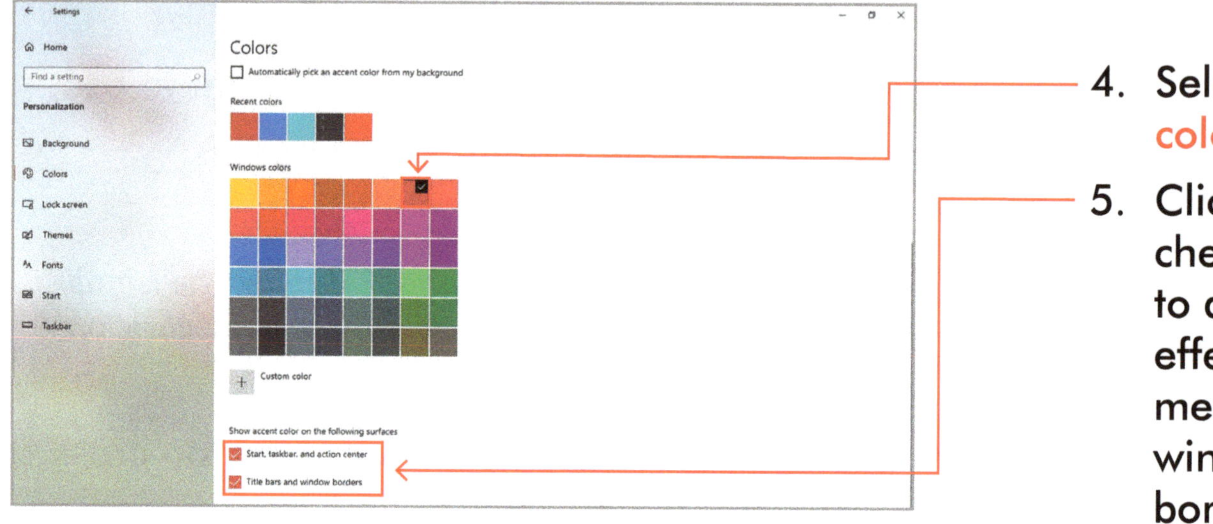

4. Select any colour.
5. Click these two check boxes to apply color effect on Start menu,Taskbar, window borders,etc.

APPLYING THEME

A theme is a combination of desktop background pictures, Windows colours scheme, screen saver and sound. Each theme includes its own set of desktop icons, sound effects and mouse pointers. To apply a theme, follow these steps:

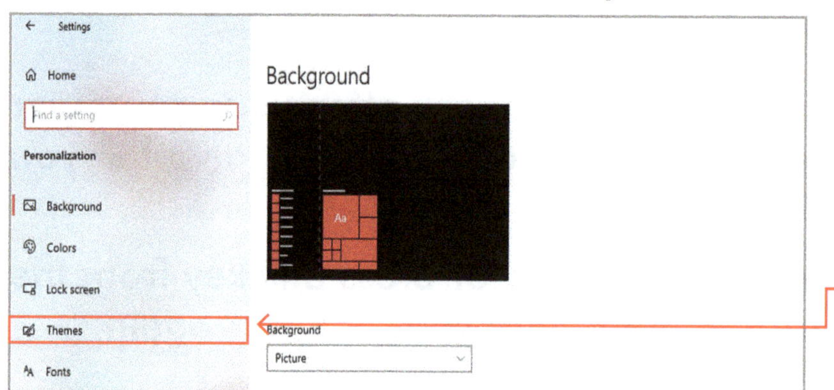

1. Open the Personalization window.
2. Click on Themes.

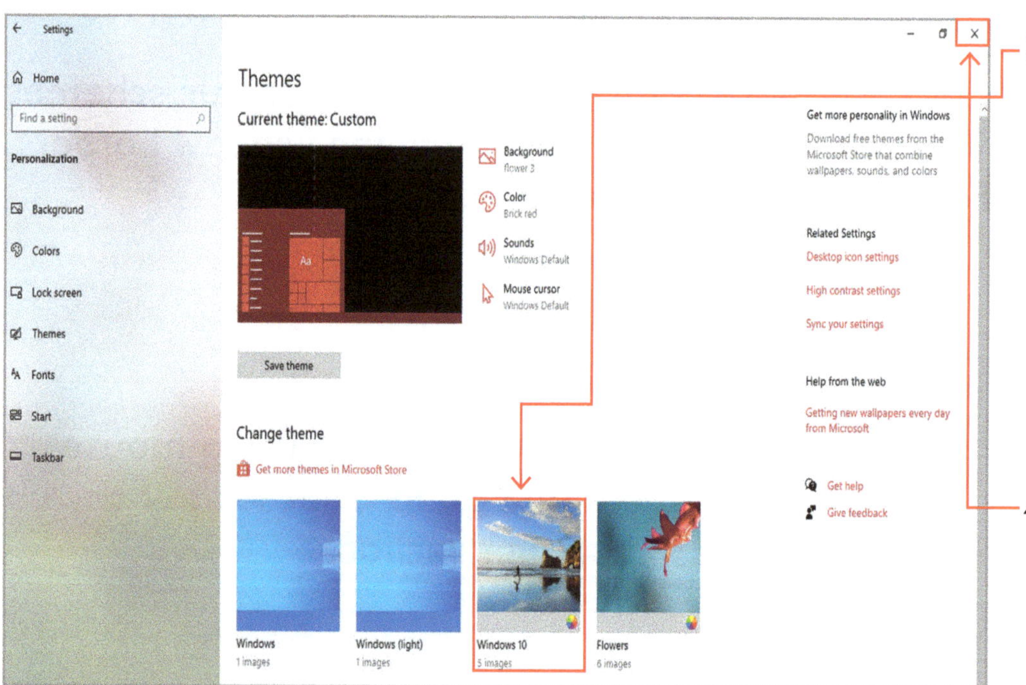

3. Click on any of the themes from the available list.

   Window 10 applies the theme.

   You can see the immediate effect on the Desktop.
4. Click on Close (×) to close the Personalization window.

SETTING DESKTOP ICONS AND CHANGING ICON PICTURE

You can change the look and feel of desktop icons.

1. Select Themes.
2. Go to the Related Settings section.
3. Select Desktop icon Settings. Desktop icon Settings dialog box will appear.

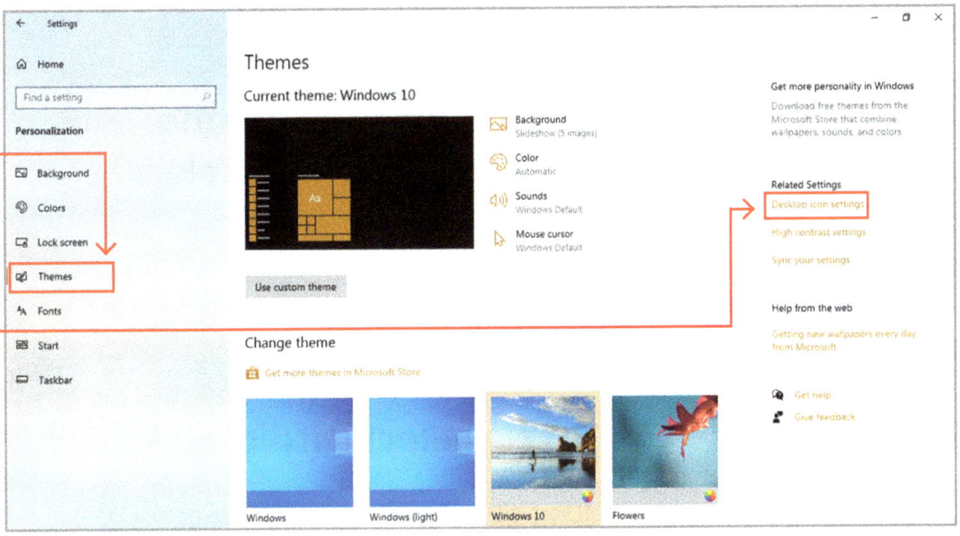

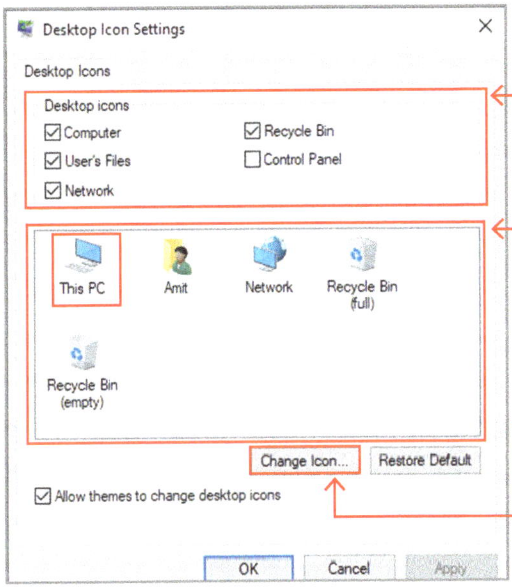

Check the boxes of related icons that you want to display on the Desktop.

4. Select the icon to change the picture.
5. Select Change Icon.

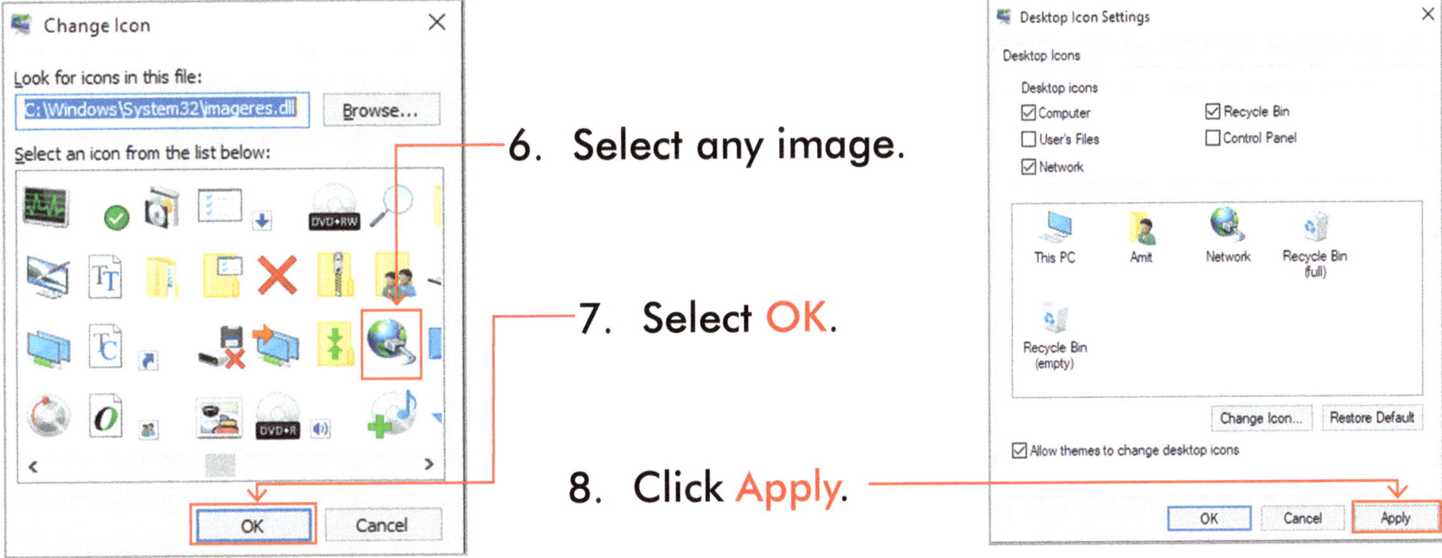

6. Select any image.
7. Select OK.
8. Click Apply.

CHANGING FONT SIZE AND ICON SIZE

We can enlarge the size of the fonts and icons of our window. By default, the size is set to 100%.

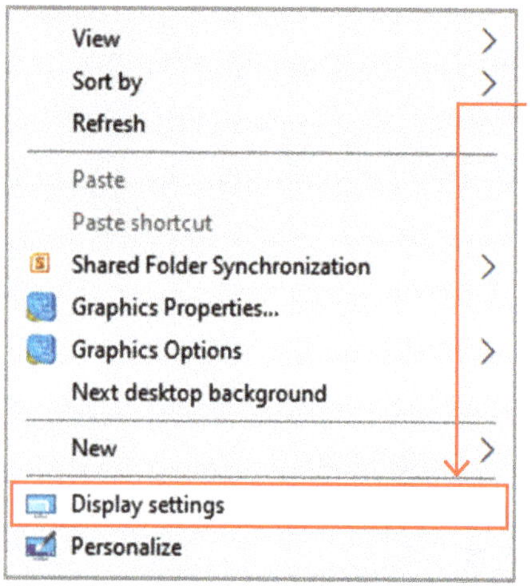

1. Right-click on the desktop and select Display Settings.
2. Select Display.
3. Click and select the required option from the list. 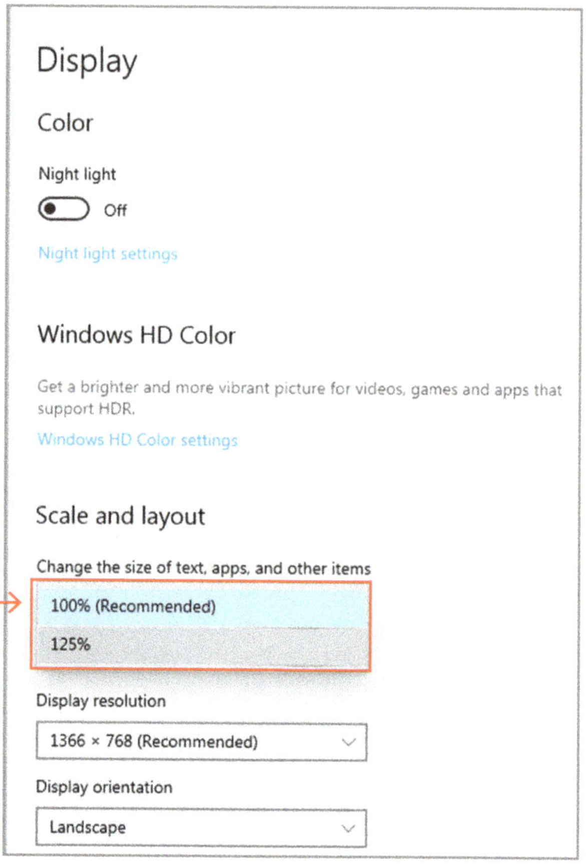

CHANGING ACCOUNT PICTURE

With Windows 10, everyone who uses your computer can have his/her own user account and each account can have a different picture. Let's learn to change the account picture.

1. Right-click on the desktop, and select Personalize option window. Personalize Settings window will appear.

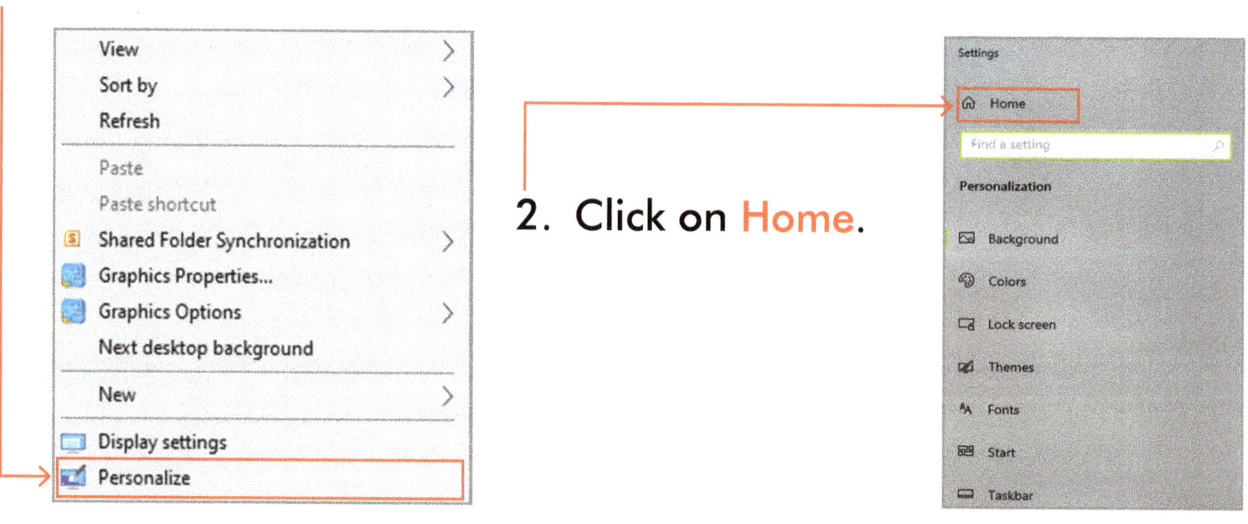

2. Click on Home.

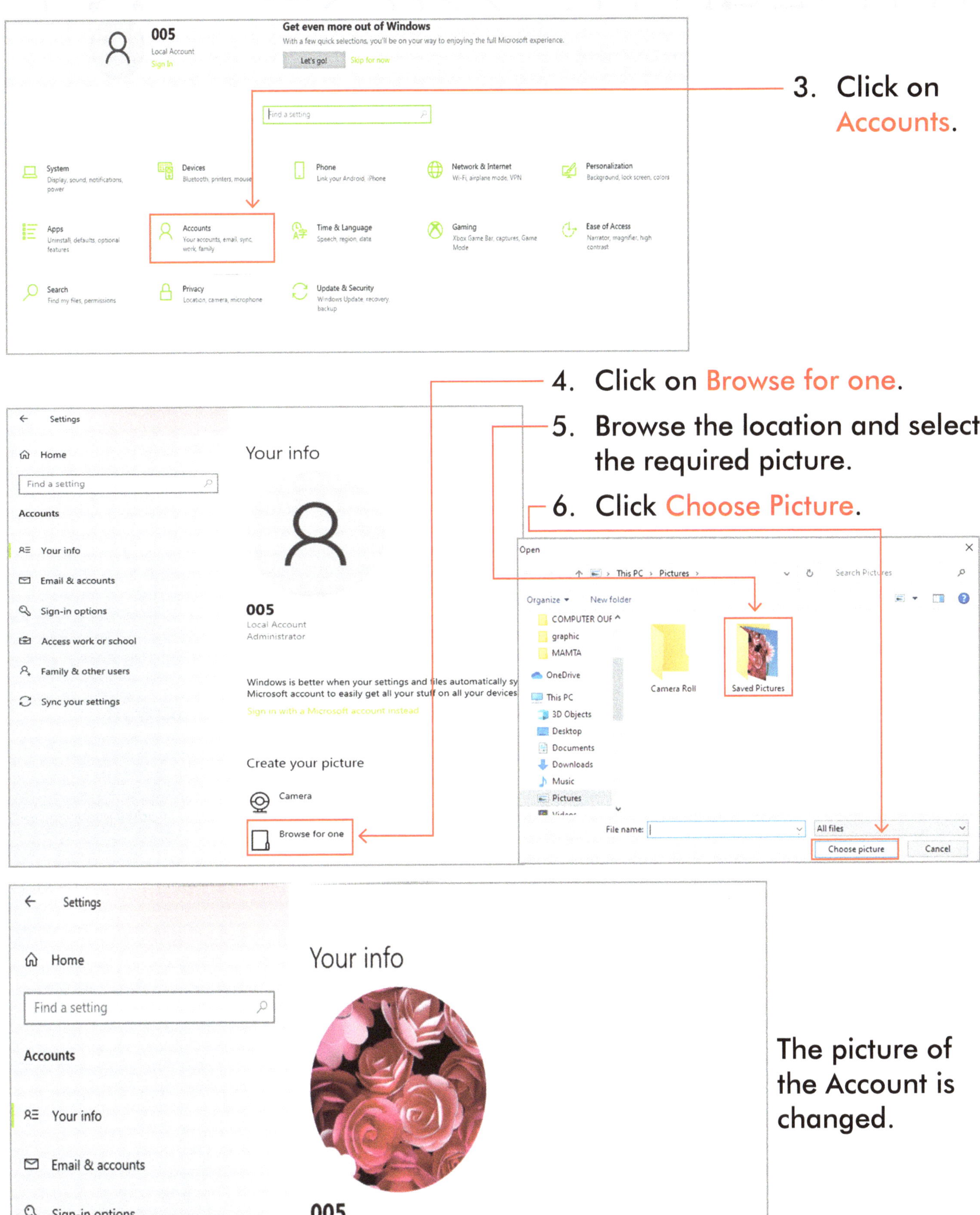

3. Click on **Accounts**.

4. Click on **Browse for one**.

5. Browse the location and select the required picture.

6. Click **Choose Picture**.

The picture of the Account is changed.

LET'S HAVE A LOOK

- You can personalize your desktop by changing the background and themes.
- To change the background you can change the wallpaper.
- A screen saver is the moving image on the screen that appears when the computer has been left untouched for a particular period of time.
- A Theme is a combination of background, colour scheme, screen saver and sound.
- Change desktop icons and display option of Personalization window help to change the icon picture and icon size respectively.

BRAIN TEASER

1. Answer the following questions:

a. How can you personalize a desktop?

____

____

____

b. Write the different picture options of the image on a screen.

____

____

____

c. What is a screen saver? How is it helpful?

____

____

____

d. What is a theme?

____

____

____

2. Answer each of the following in one word or line:

a. Which window is used to open every time in order to decorate a desktop?

____

b. Name the picture position option that displays a single copy of the image extended on all sides.

____

c. What is Lock screen?

____

3. Multiple Choice Questions

Tick (✓) the correct answer:

a. The option that displays a single copy of the image extended to all sides

i. Tile ☐ ii. Stretch ☐ iii. Center ☐

b. A moving image that appears when the computer has been left untouched for some time

i. Background ☐ ii. Screen saver ☐ iii. Desktop ☐

c. Combination of desktop background, colour, screen saver and sound

i. Wallpaper ☐ ii. Theme ☐ iii. Taskbar ☐

4. Write 'T' for true and 'F' for false in the boxes:

a. You can change the desktop background. ☐

b. A control panel is used to open the disk drives. ☐

c. You cannot add your own picture to a desktop background. ☐

d. The screen saver appears when the computer has been left untouched for some time. ☐

e. We can change the background by changing the wallpaper. ☐

f. Accounts option in Windows Settings window helps to change account picture. ☐

5. Write the steps for:

a. Changing desktop background.

b. Changing an account picture.

Visit your computer lab and apply the steps to change the background setting, the screen saver and applying themes.

Save your photograph on your home computer and set it as a wallpaper on the desktop.

TO THE TEACHER

Let the students change the background setting but keep on watching that they do not disturb the other setting of the computer.

6 Word Processor

Dear friends, after decorating the desktop of the computer, let's move further and learn to type accurately and efficiently in the computer. In the previous class you learnt to type in a Word Processor, MS-Word. In this class, you will be learning some more about it.

WORD PROCESSOR

A word processor is an application software program that enables you to type your text in a computer. The process of typing using word processor is known as Word Processing.

Word Processor has replaced the electronic typewriter in most offices because you can easily change what they have written with word processor. A word processor is formally known as document preparation system.

Millions of people use word processing softwares every day to develop documents such as letters, memos, reports, newsletters and Web pages. It also has many features to make documents look professional and visually appealing.

There are many word processing software available. Some of them are:

⇒ **Microsoft Word :** One of the most well-known and widely used word processing applications is Microsoft Word.

⇒ **Microsoft Works :** It is also one of the most well-known word processing applications created by Microsoft for Macintosh PCs and Windows.

⇒ **Lotus Word Pro :** This word processor software, produced by IBM, allows you to create and distribute formatted text documents.

⇒ **Adobe InCopy :** It is a professional word processing software product made by Adobe Systems.

Features of Word Processor

The following are the word processing features used in the processing of the document:

⇒ You can edit words and sentences.

⇒ You can change the size and style of letters and make them colourful.

⇒ You can set the margins for your page.

⇒ You can cut, copy and paste text within the document or another document.

⇒ You can check and correct spellings and grammatical errors.

⇒ You can insert graphics in your document.

⇒ You can create form letters, mailing labels and envelopes.

⇒ You can correct common spellings and capitalisation errors by using the AutoCorrect feature.

⇒ You can Find and Replace certain characters, words or phrases.

⇒ You can use a synonym (word with the same meaning) for a word in a document.

⇒ You can save your work for future use.

⇒ You can print your document.

There are many other features of word processor, but this should be enough to get you started.

WORD PROCESSOR

Microsoft Word or MS-Word is the word processor software. It has all the features that a good word processor should have. It allows the user to type, edit, format and print the text in a document. It is an application which is used for creating documents. Let's start working on it.

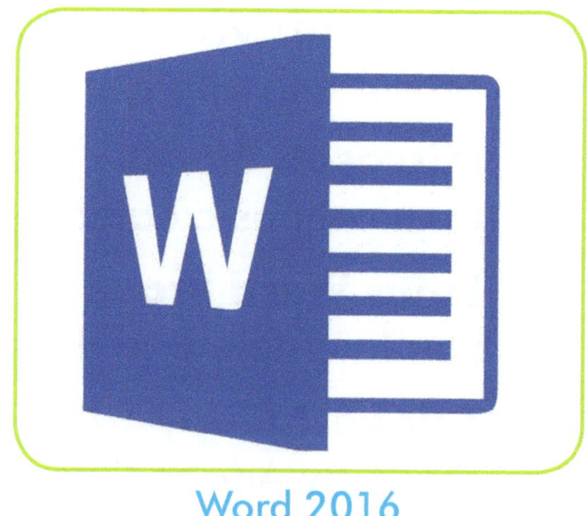

Word 2016

STARTING WORD 2016

Before working in MS-Word, first you should know how to open Word window. Follow the steps as mentioned below to open the Word window.

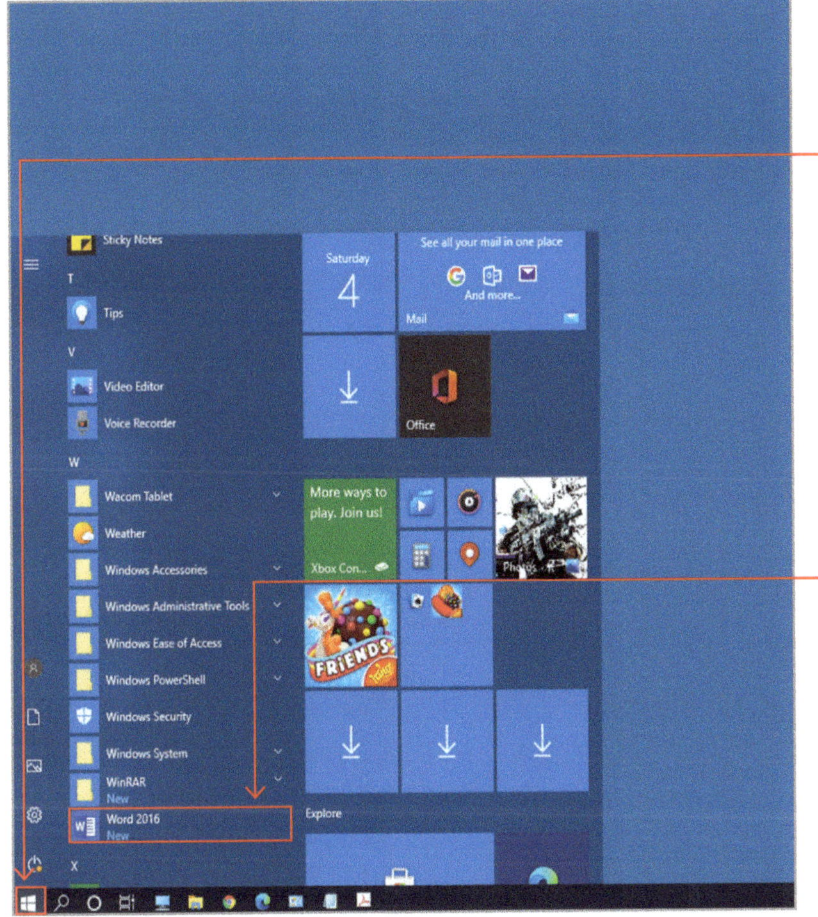

1. Click on the Start button. The Start menu will appear.
2. Scroll the menu and go to W section.
3. Click on Word 2016.

   The Word window will appear.

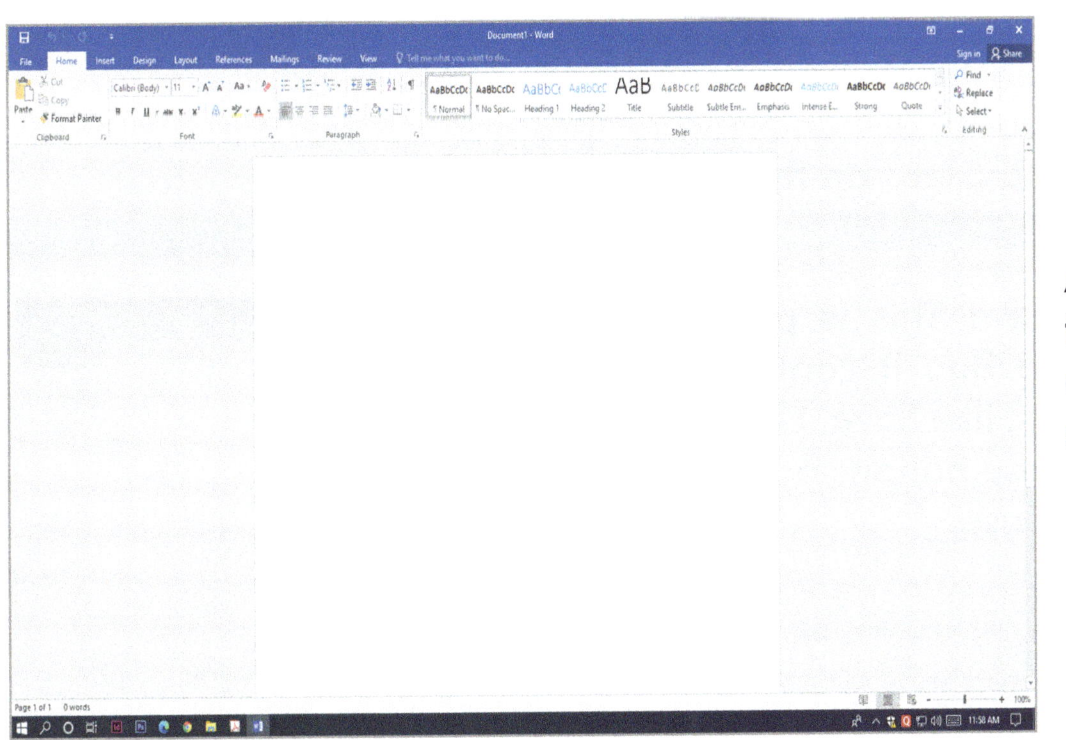

An empty document titled Document 1 appears on your screen.

COMPONENTS OF MS-WORD WINDOW

After starting the MS-Word you will get a window on your desktop which displays many items you can use to create and work with your documents.

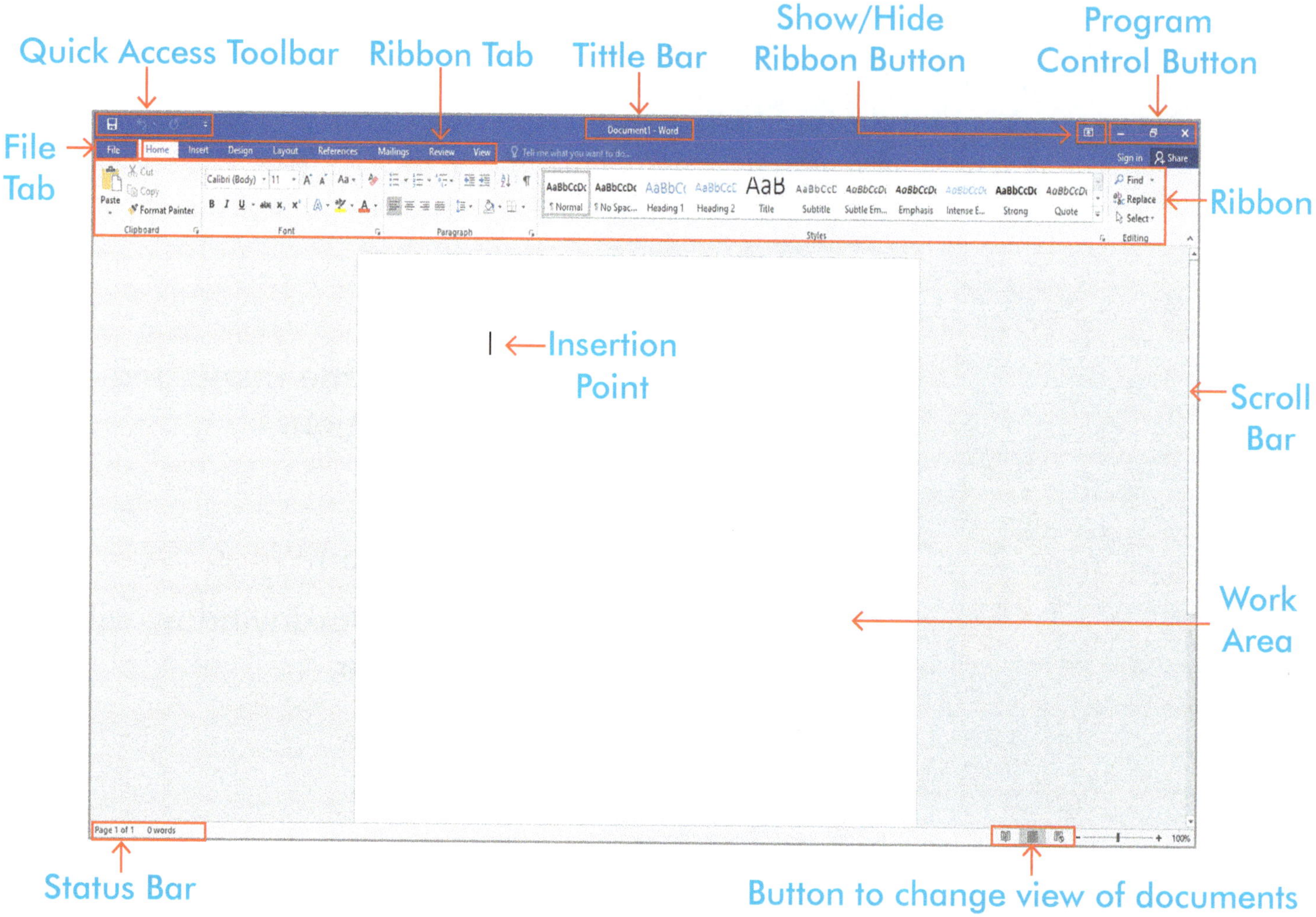

Quick Access Toolbar
Ribbon Tab
Tittle Bar
Show/Hide Ribbon Button
Program Control Button
File Tab
Ribbon
Insertion Point
Scroll Bar
Work Area
Status Bar
Button to change view of documents

Title Bar : This is the bar that is present at the top of MS-Word. It displays the name of the current document and current program. It has three buttons: Minimize, Maximize and Close on the left corner.

Document1 - Word

Quick Access Toolbar : This is present on the left corner of the Title Bar. It contains the most commonly used buttons, like Save, Undo, Redo and Repeat commands. These buttons activate with just a single click of the mouse.

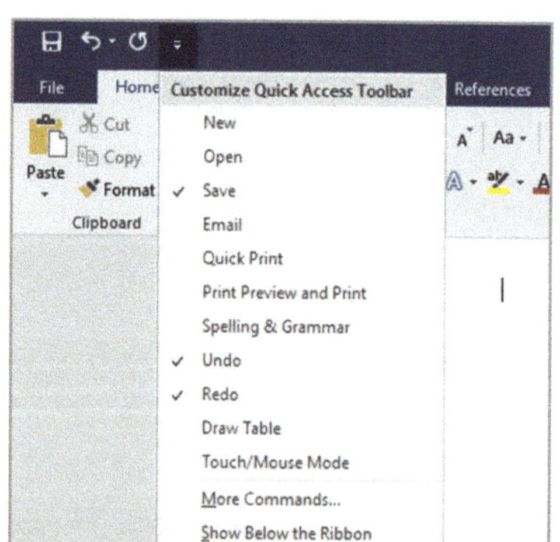

To Minimize and Maximize the Ribbon

The Ribbon is designed to respond to your current task, but you can choose to minimize the Ribbon, if you find that it takes up too much of the screen space.

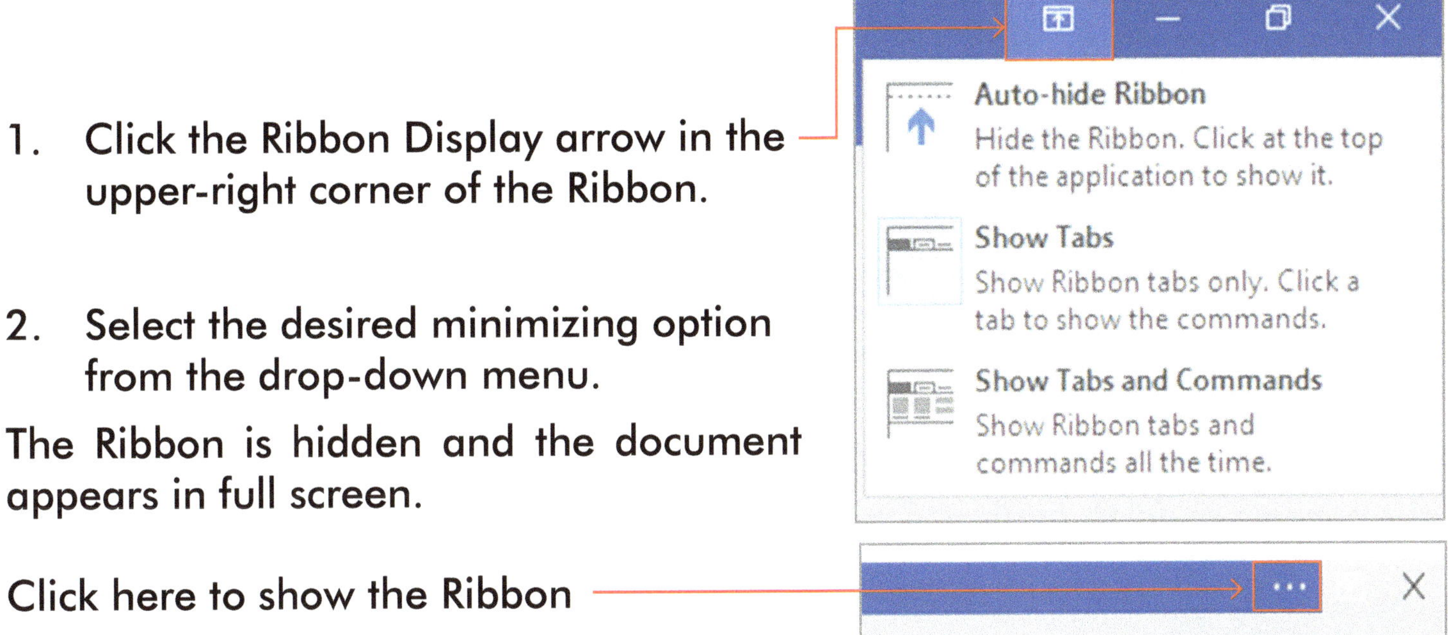

1. Click the Ribbon Display arrow in the upper-right corner of the Ribbon.
2. Select the desired minimizing option from the drop-down menu.

The Ribbon is hidden and the document appears in full screen.

Click here to show the Ribbon

File Tab : Under the Quick Access Toolbar, the first button on the left side is the File tab which shows the Backstage view. In the Backstage view, the file information can be managed, like save, share, print, protect and work with the version information for document.

⇒ The Backstage view that appears is organized in three panels: the left, centre and right panel. For example, when you click on Print in the First panel, the second or centre panel shows print options. The third or right panel displays a preview of your document as it will appear in print.

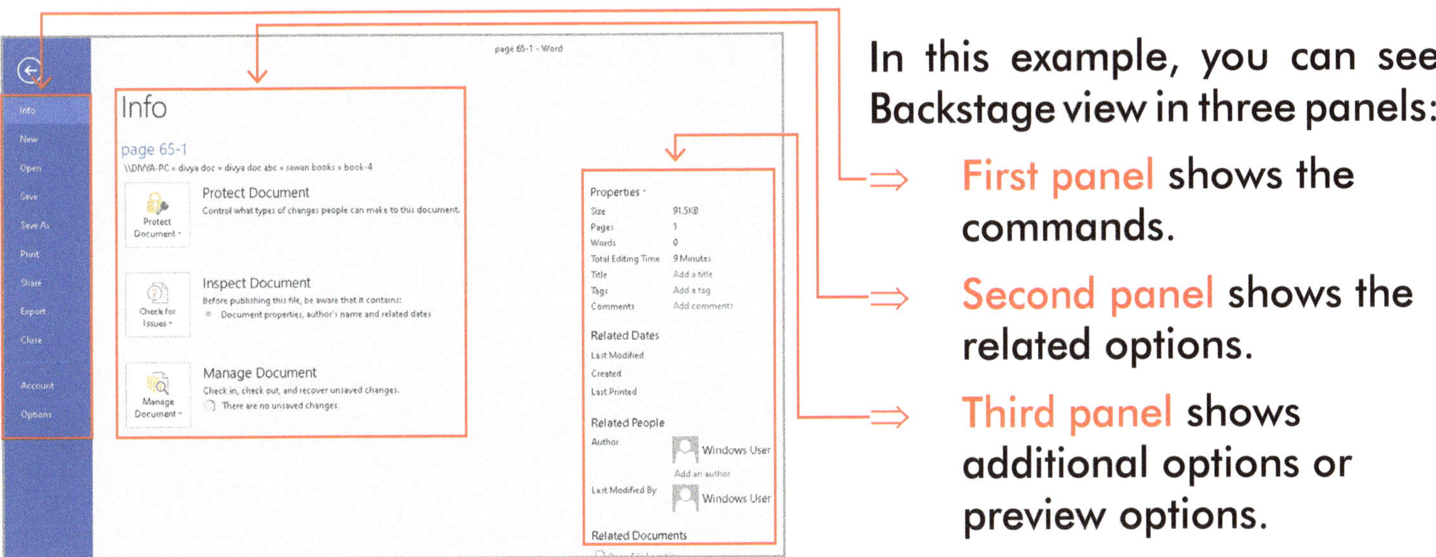

In this example, you can see Backstage view in three panels:

⇒ First panel shows the commands.

⇒ Second panel shows the related options.

⇒ Third panel shows additional options or preview options.

Insertion Point: A small blinking line on the screen is known as Insertion Point. As you type the text on the screen, it keeps shifting towards the right side of the screen.

Views of Document : There are different views in Word, *i.e.* Print Layout, Full Screen Reading, Web Layout, Outline and Draft. You can access your document in these views.

Work Area : The plain white area within the window where the text is typed.

Scroll bars : You can move the text of the window vertically or horizontally up, down, right and left by using the scroll bars.

Status Bar : The Bar which shows the current status like page number, column number, zoom option, etc.

Program Window Controls : The buttons present on the right corner of the Title bar are used to minimize, maximize, restore or close the window.

RIBBON

The Ribbon replaces toolbars and menus to help you quickly find the commands to complete a task. The Ribbon consists of a group of tabs. Each tab holds a set of related commands.

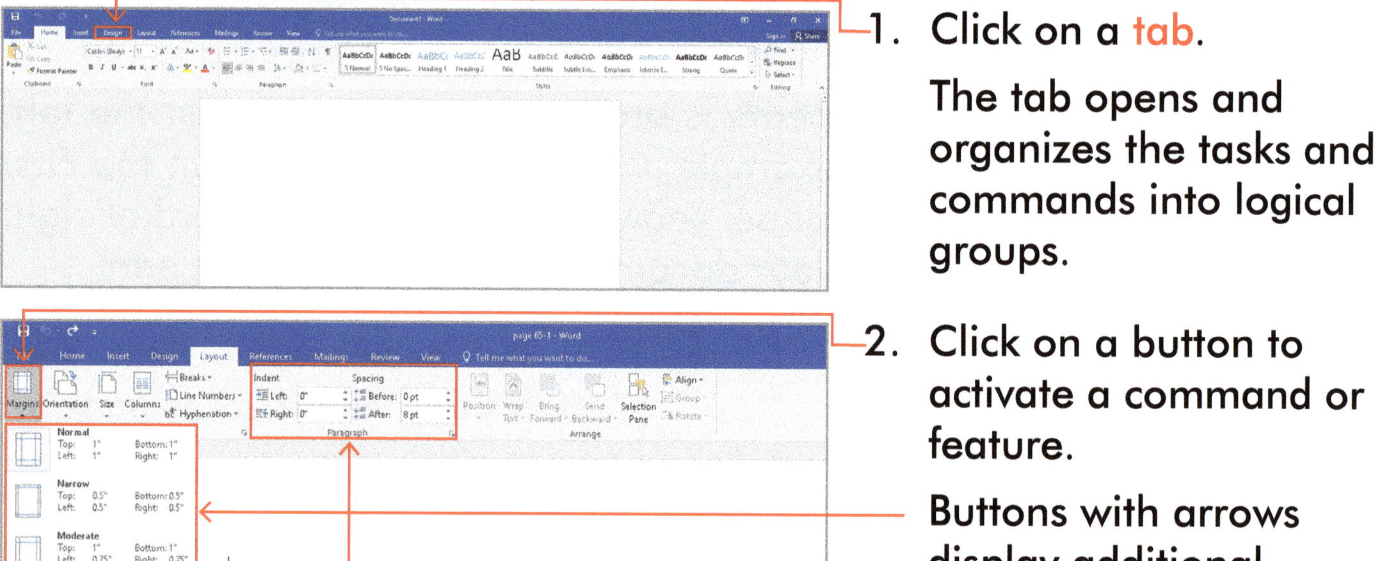

1. Click on a tab.

   The tab opens and organizes the tasks and commands into logical groups.

2. Click on a button to activate a command or feature.

   Buttons with arrows display additional commands.

   You can click on the corner arrow button to display a dialog box of additional settings.

CLOSING WORD DOCUMENT

After finishing the work, you can close the document.

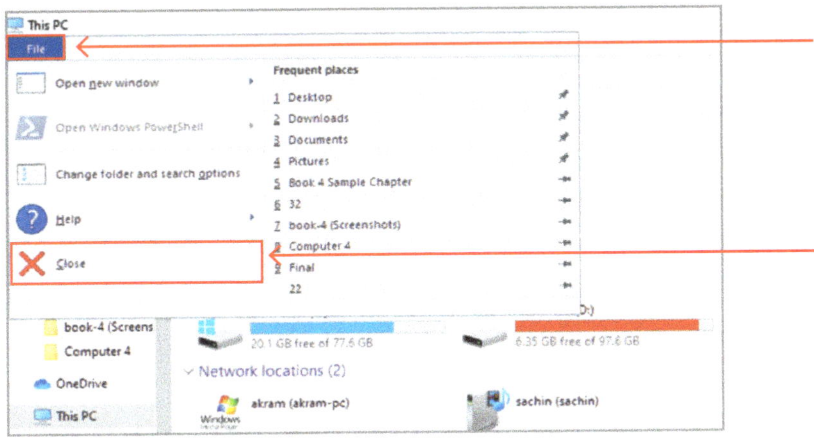

1. Click on File tab.

   Backstage view will appear.

2. Click on the Close button.

   Word closes the current open document.

EXITING FROM WORD

To exit from the Word window, click on the X button in the Program Control Buttons in the Title Bar.

LET'S HAVE A LOOK

- A word processor is an application software program that enables you to type your text in a computer.
- A word processor was formally known as document preparation system.
- One of the most well-known and widely used word processing applications is Microsoft Word.
- You can check and correct spellings and grammatical errors.
- The Backstage view is organized in three panels: the left, centre and right panel.
- Ribbon consists of a group of tabs; each tab holds a set of related commands.

BRAIN TEASER

1. Answer the following questions:

a. What is Word Processor?

b. Write any five features of Word Processor.

c. What is Backstage view?

d. What are the different components of MS-Word Window? Explain any two.

e. What is Microsoft Word?

2. Answer each of the following in one word or line:

a. Name two types of word processors.

b. Name the toolbar that contains buttons like save, undo and redo commands.

c. Write an important feature of word processor.

d. Name the different views of document in MS-Word.

e. Name the toolbar that is present on the left corner of title bar.

3. Fill in the blanks:

a. The process of typing using a word processor is known as __________.

b. A word processor was formally known as __________.

c. __________ is word processor software produced by IBM.

d. __________ is a word processing application from Adobe System.

e. __________ is the bar that is present at the top of MS-Word.

f. The Ribbon contains two parts: __________ and __________.

4. Write 'T' for true and 'F' for false in the boxes:

a. Word processor is used to type text using the keyboard. ☐

b. MS-Word is an example of Word processor. ☐

c. You cannot save text in MS-Word. ☐

d. The title bar displays the name of the currently active document. ☐

e. The Ribbon is the area where you enter the text. ☐

f. Backstage view has five panels. ☐

g. Insertion Point is a blinking line on the screen. ☐

5. Multiple Choice Questions

Tick (✓) the correct answer:

a. The program used to create, store and print the document

i. Word editor ☐

ii. LOGO ☐

iii. Word Processor ☐

b. The word processing program that allows you to create text document.

i. Paint ☐

ii. MS-Word ☐

iii. Adobe Photoshop ☐

c. The blinking line on the screen is

i. Mouse pointer ☐ ii. Insertion Point ☐ iii. Ribbon ☐

d. The plain white area within the window where the text is typed

i. Work Area ☐ ii. Ribbon ☐ iii. Scroll Bar ☐

e. The bar on the left corner of the title bar is

i. Control bar ☐

ii. Ribbon ☐

iii. Quick Access Toolbar ☐

6. Label the following:

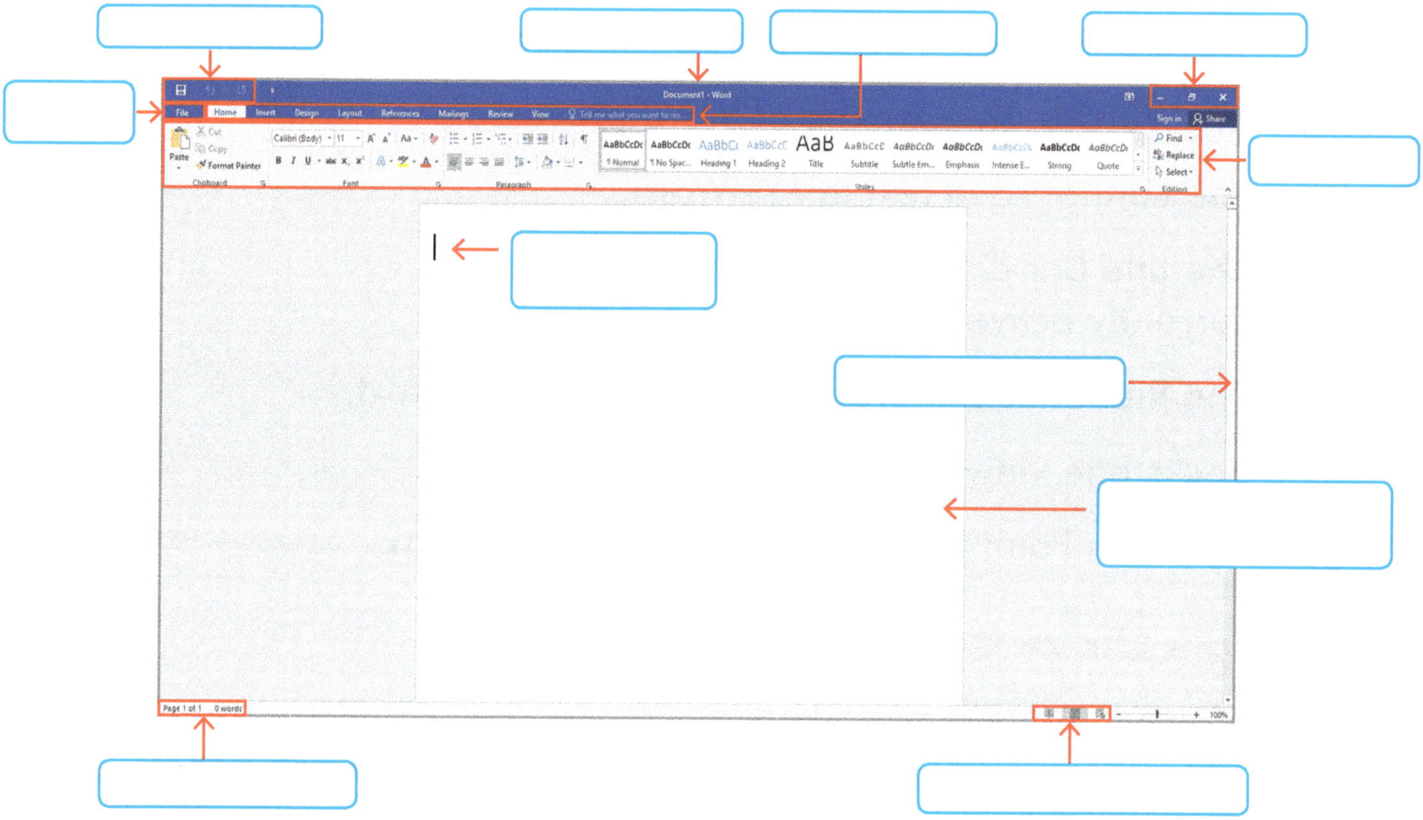

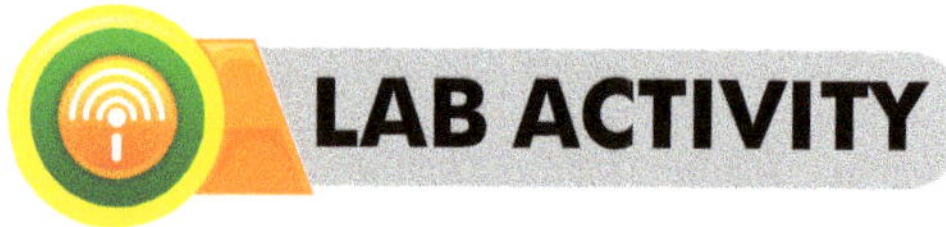

LAB ACTIVITY

Visit your computer lab. Open MS-Word window and explore the ribbon tabs on the ribbon. Also, try to see the Backstage view and observe what you have studied.

7 Working With Ms-Word

Hello students! Now you are quite familiar with MS-Word 2016 window and its different elements. Now in this chapter, we will start working in it and create a document using its different features.

MS-WORD

Microsoft Word (MS-Word) is a Word processing program that enables you to create document. MS-Word 2016 is the latest version of Microsoft Word.

CREATING A NEW DOCUMENT

You can create a new document in Word any time you want to write a piece of new text. Creating a new document is just like opening your notebook and start writing on a fresh and new piece of paper every time.

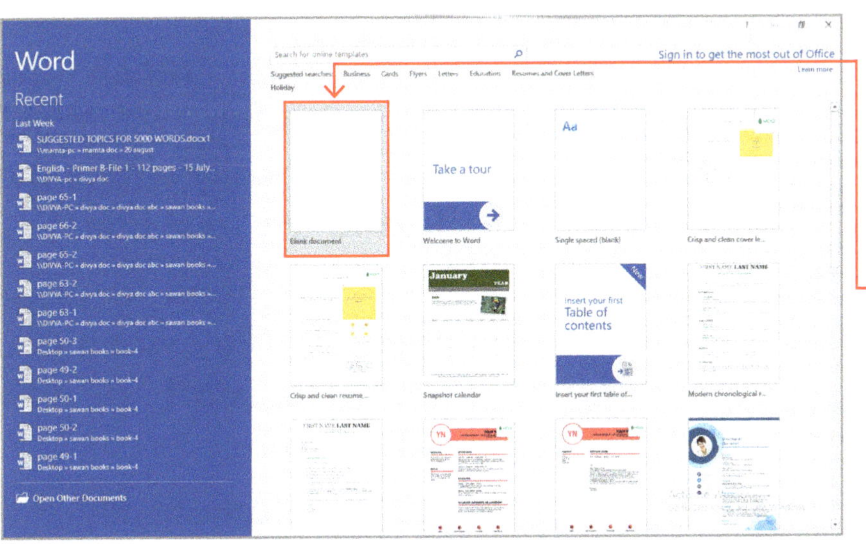

1. Click on File tab.

   Backstage view will appear.
2. Click on the New button.
3. Click on Blank Document in the Templates list.

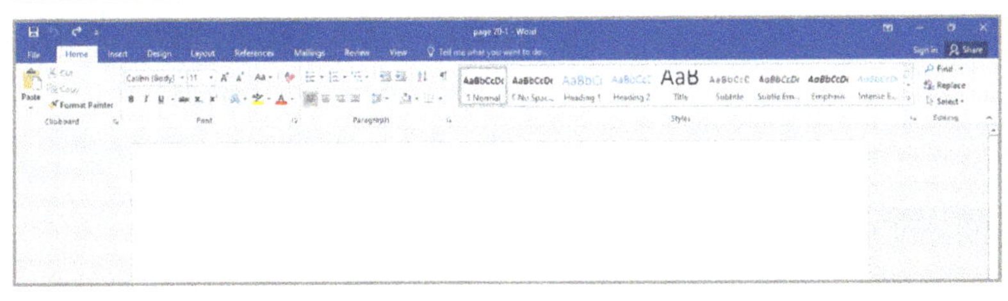

The new document file opens, and you can start adding your own data.

Entering Text in Word

The text can be entered into a document with the help of a keyboard. The typed text will appear where the insertion point (cursor) flashes on the screen.

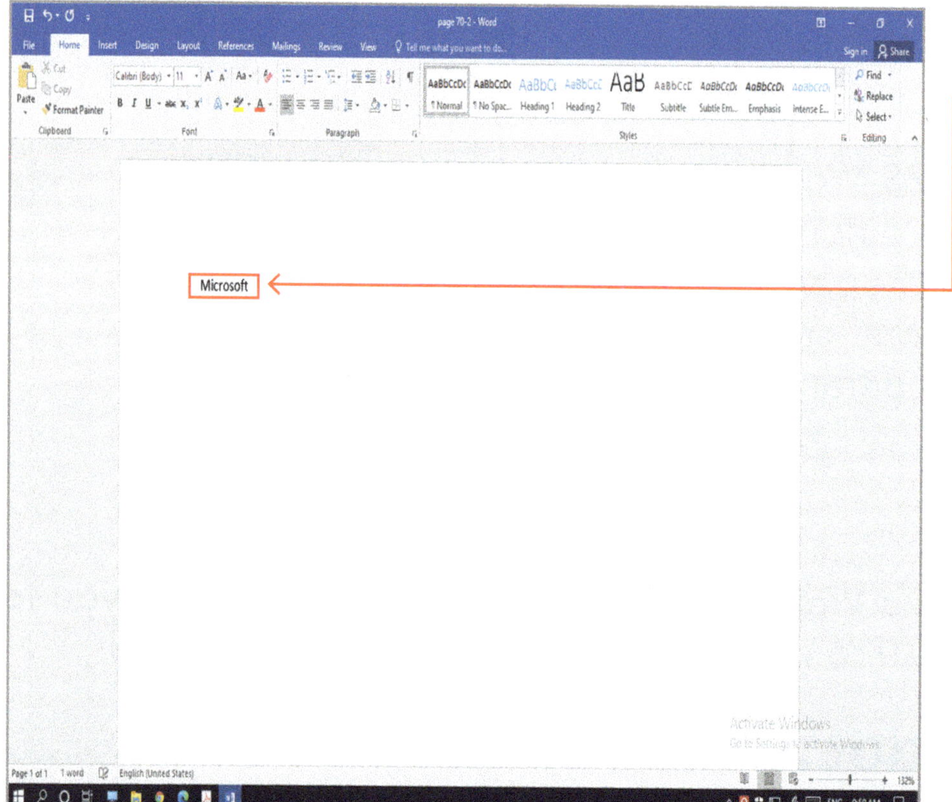

Type in the document where you see the cursor or insertion point.

Do you know 

MS-Word knows where the margins are. Just keep typing and the Word will automatically organize the text within the margins.

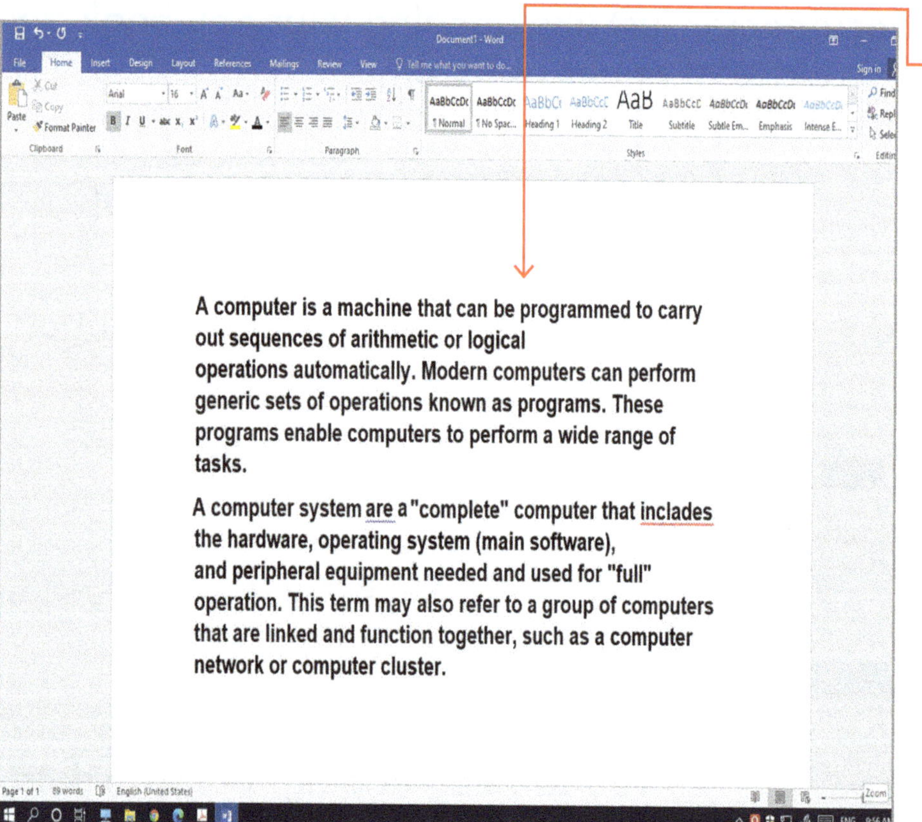

1. Type the text for your document.

   When you reach the end of a line, MS-Word automatically wraps the text to the next line.

   You only need to press the Enter key when you want to start a new paragraph.

   Word automatically underlines mis-spelled words in red and grammar errors in blue.

Saving a Document

The user can save a new document after creating it so that it may be used for future reference. To save the document, you have to follow the steps:

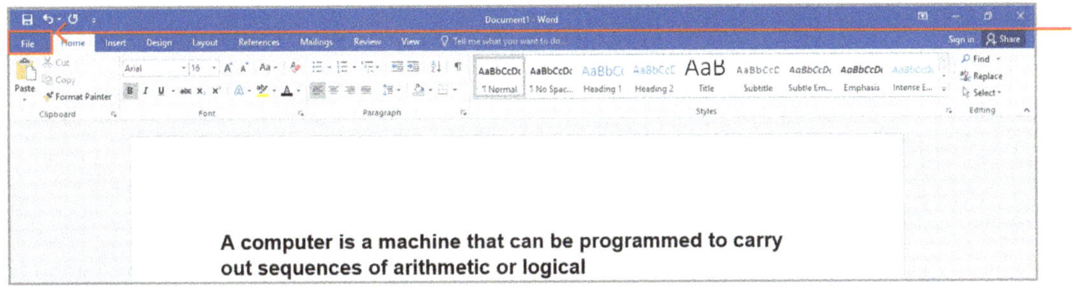

1. Click on File tab. Backstage view will appear.

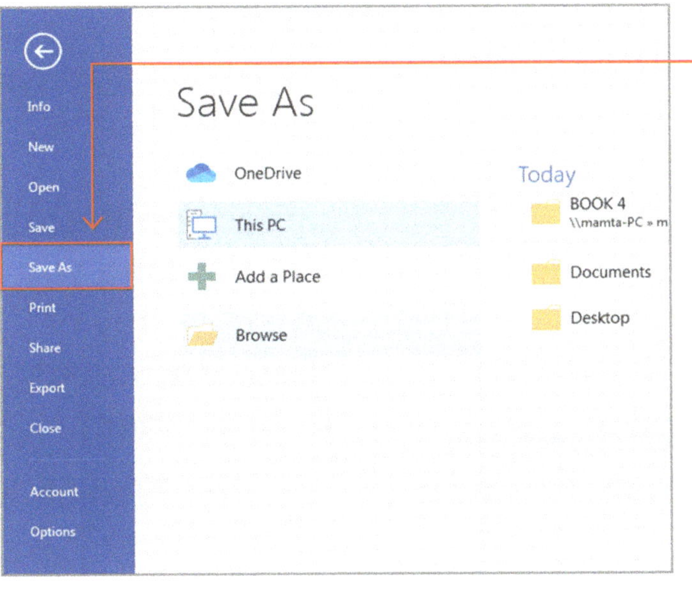

2. Click on the Save or Save As button.

   The Save As dialog box appears.

You can click the Save button on Quick Access toolbar to save the file.

3. Click on these areas to navigate to the folder in which you want to save the file. Choose the location. In this example, Desktop is selected.
4. Click in the File name text box and type a name (Computer) for the file.
5. Click on Save.

The Keyboard shortcut to save a document is Ctrl+S.

The Word saves the file and the new file name appears on the title bar.

Opening an Existing Document

Suppose a user has already created a document in MS-Word and the document is saved in the form of files on your computer. When you want to edit or see a document, you can open an existing document.

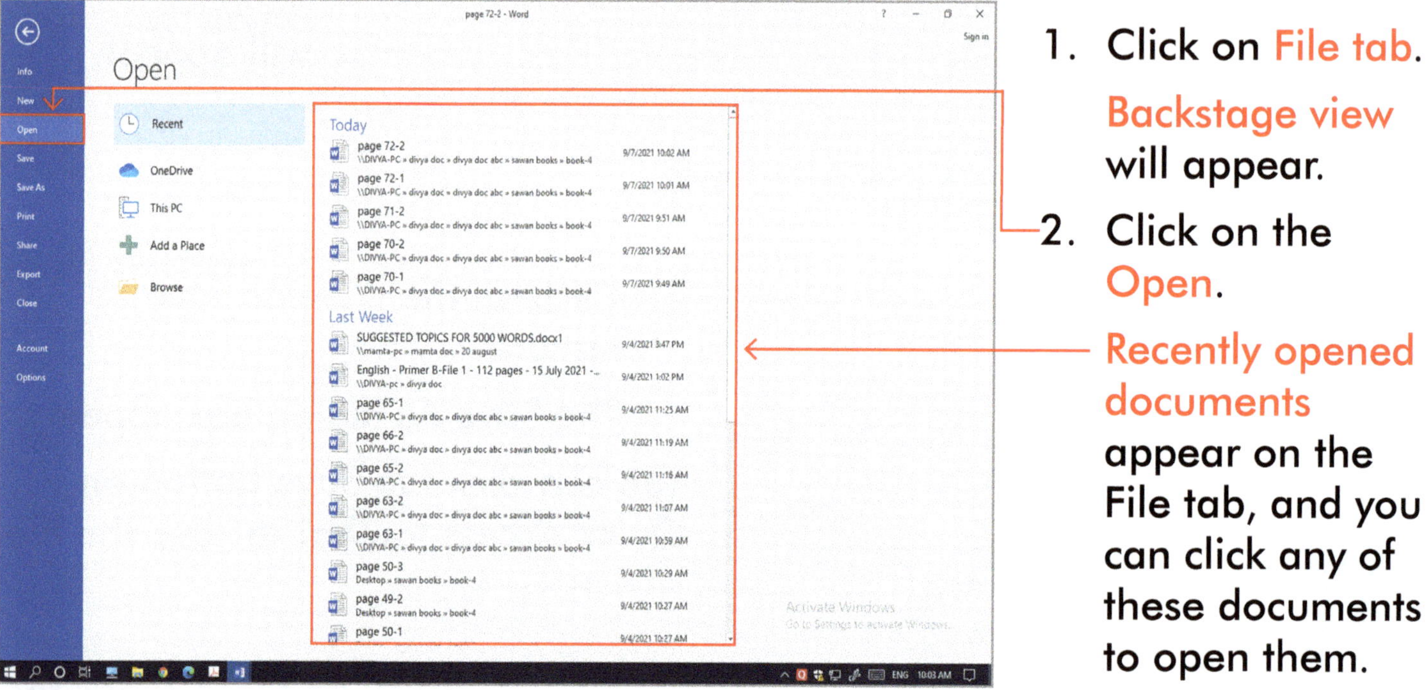

1. Click on File tab. Backstage view will appear.
2. Click on the Open.

Recently opened documents appear on the File tab, and you can click any of these documents to open them.

If the document is not seen in Recent documents, select This PC and then click on Browse.

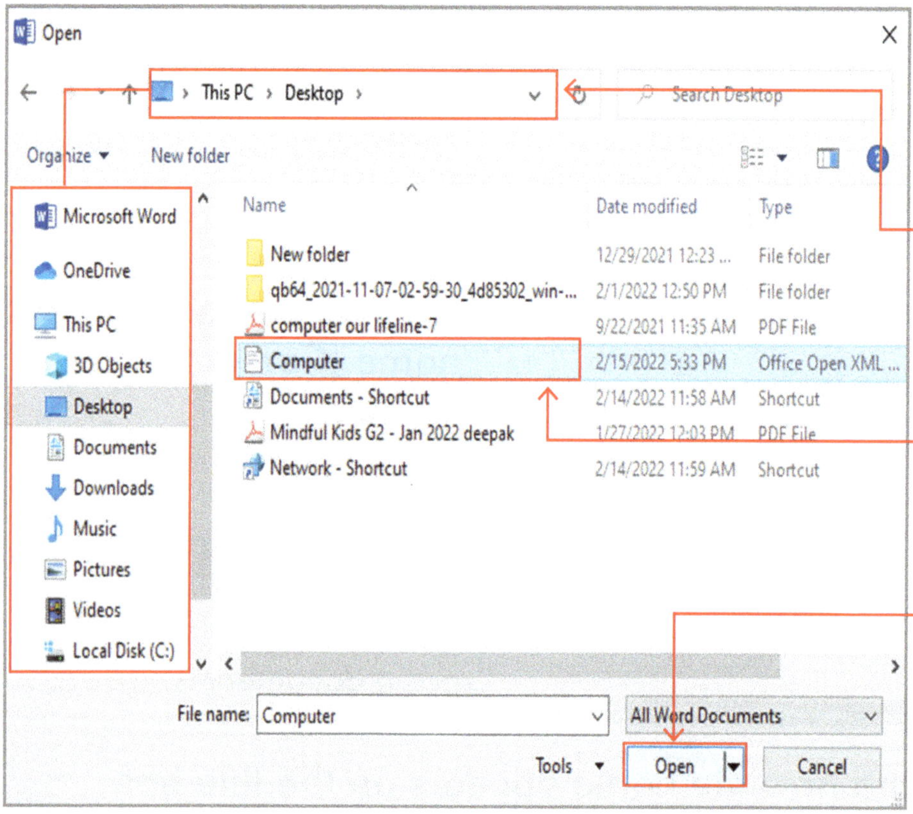

The Open dialog box appears.

3. Click on these areas to navigate to the folder or drive where you stored the file.
4. Click on the name of the file that you want to open.
5. Click on Open.

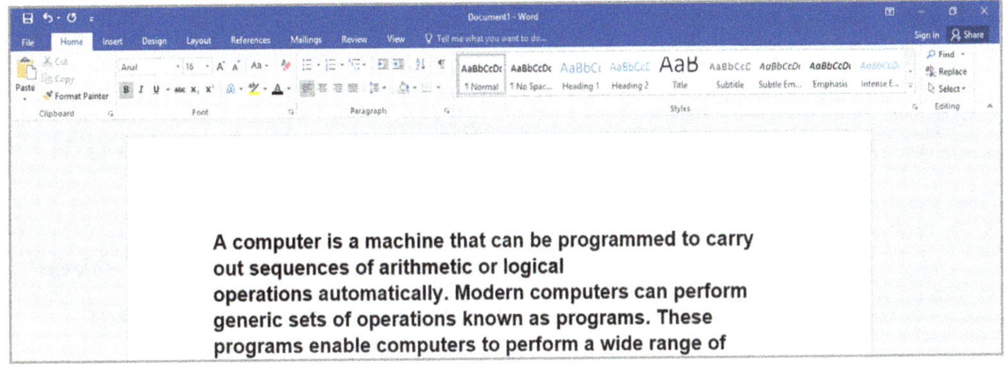

The file opens in the program window.

The keyboard shortcut to open a document is Ctrl+O.

SELECTING TEXT

You can select the whole text or a part of text according to your need. Selected text appears highlighted on the screen. To select a piece of text or a lot of text, follow these steps:

Selecting a Word

A computer is a machine that can be programmed to carry out sequences of arithmetic or logical operations automatically. Modern computers can perform generic sets of operations known as programs. These programs enable computers to perform a wide range of tasks.

A computer system is a» complete «computer that includes the hardware, operating system) main software), and peripheral equipment needed and used for» full «operation. This term may also refer to a group of computers that are linked and function together, such as a computer network or computer cluster.

A broad range of industrial and consumer products use computers as control systems. Simple special-purpose devices like microwave ovens and remote controls are included, as are factory devices like industrial robots and computer-aided design, as well as general-purpose devices like personal computers and mobile devices like smartphones. Computers power the Internet, which links hundreds of millions of other computers and users.

1. Double-click the word you want to select.

   The word will be selected.

   To deselect text, click outside the selected area.

Selecting a Sentence

A computer is a machine that can be programmed to carry out sequences of arithmetic or logical operations automatically. Modern computers can perform generic sets of operations known as programs. These programs enable computers to perform a wide range of tasks.

A computer system is a» complete «computer that includes the hardware, operating system) main software), and peripheral equipment needed and used for» full «operation. This term may also refer to a group of computers that are linked and function together, such as a computer network or computer cluster.

A broad range of industrial and consumer products use computers as control systems. Simple special-purpose devices like microwave ovens and remote controls are included, as are factory devices like industrial robots and computer-aided design, as well as general-purpose devices like personal computers and mobile devices like smartphones. Computers power the Internet, which links hundreds of millions of other computers and users.

1. Press and hold down the Ctrl key from the keyboard.
2. Still holding down the Ctrl key, click the sentence you want to select.

Selecting a Paragraph

A computer is a machine that can be programmed to carry out sequences of arithmetic or logical operations automatically. Modern computers can perform generic sets of operations known as programs. These programs enable computers to perform a wide range of tasks.

A computer system is a» complete «computer that includes the hardware, operating system) main software), and peripheral equipment needed and used for» full «operation. This term may also refer to a group of computers that are linked and function together, such as a computer network or computer cluster.

A broad range of industrial and consumer products use computers as control systems. Simple special-purpose devices like microwave ovens and remote controls are included, as are factory devices like industrial robots and computer-aided design, as well as general-purpose devices like personal computers and mobile devices like smartphones. Computers power the Internet, which links hundreds of millions of other computers and users.

1. Place your mouse pointer over the paragraph and then quickly click three times to select a paragraph.

   The whole paragraph will be selected.

Selecting any amount of Text

A computer is a machine that can be programmed to carry out sequences of arithmetic or logical operations automatically. Modern computers can perform generic sets of operations known as programs. These programs enable computers to perform a wide range of tasks.

A computer system is a» complete «computer that includes the hardware, operating system) main software), and peripheral equipment needed and used for» full «operation. This term may also refer to a group of computers that are linked and function together, such as a computer network or computer cluster.

A broad range of industrial and consumer products use computers as control systems. Simple special-purpose devices like microwave ovens and remote controls are included, as are factory devices like industrial robots and computer-aided design, as well as general-purpose devices like personal computers and mobile devices like smartphones. Computers power the Internet, which links hundreds of millions of other computers and users.

1. Place your mouse pointer over the first word you want to select.
2. Drag the mouse pointer over the text you want to select.

Do you know ?

Shift key and Arrow keys can also be used from the keyboard to select text.

MOVING AND COPYING TEXT

Sometimes you are required to write a word or sentence many times. In MS-Word, you can use the same sentence any number of times very easily without typing it again and again.

Moving a text means removing or cutting the text from the original position and placing it to the other location. Copying the text will take the text to another place. Also, the text will remain to the original place.

You can use the Clipboard group in the Home tab for copy or cut the text from one place to another.

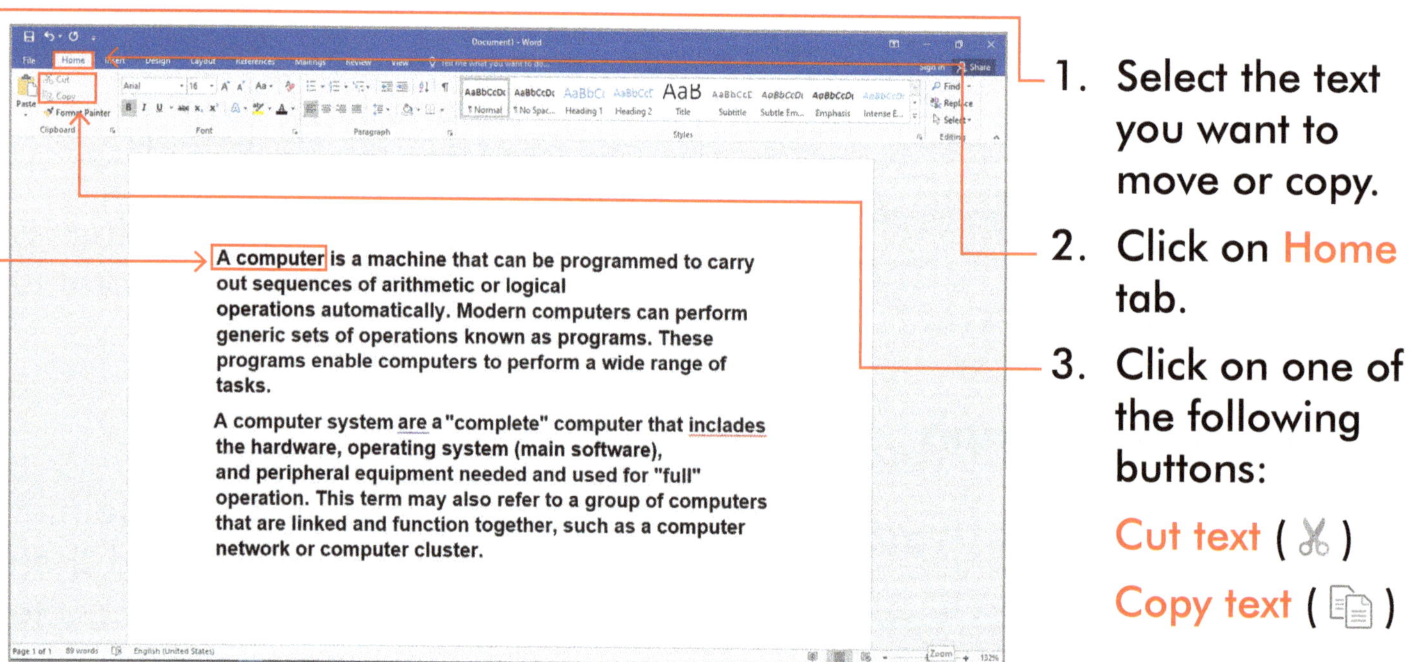

1. Select the text you want to move or copy.
2. Click on Home tab.
3. Click on one of the following buttons:

   Cut text (✂)

   Copy text (📋)

In this example, we choose Copy text so that the text may remain in its original location.

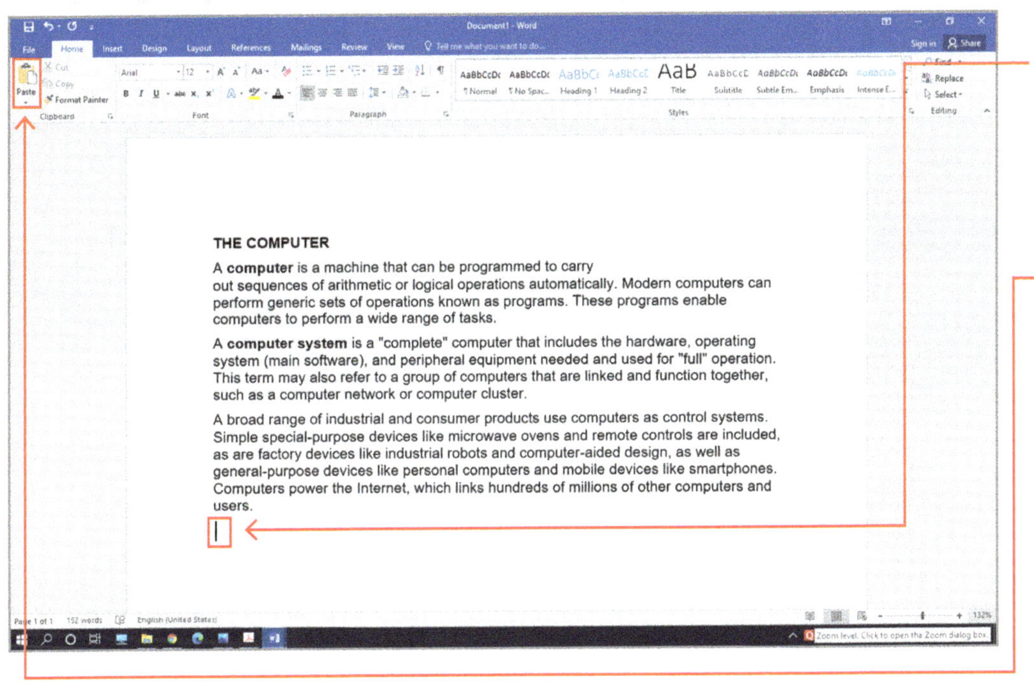

4. Click on the location where you want to place the text.
5. Click on **Paste** button ( ) to place the text in the new location.

   The text will appear in the new location.

FORMATTING A DOCUMENT

Formatting means changing and arranging text in a document to make it attractive. We can format our document mainly by using **Font** group and **Paragraph** group in the **Home** tab.

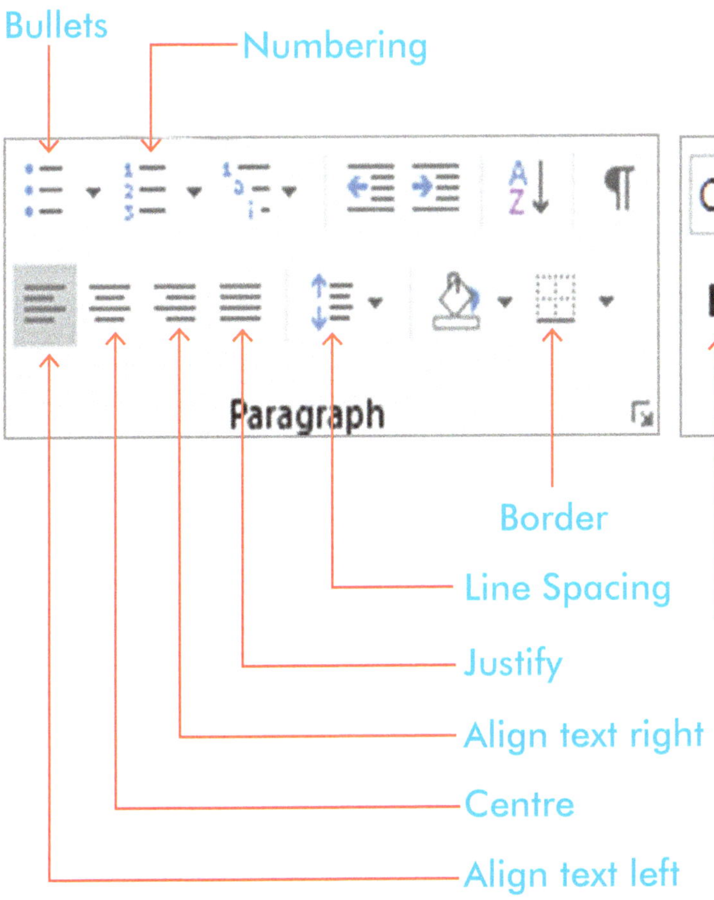

Bullets
Numbering
Paragraph
Border
Line Spacing
Justify
Align text right
Centre
Align text left

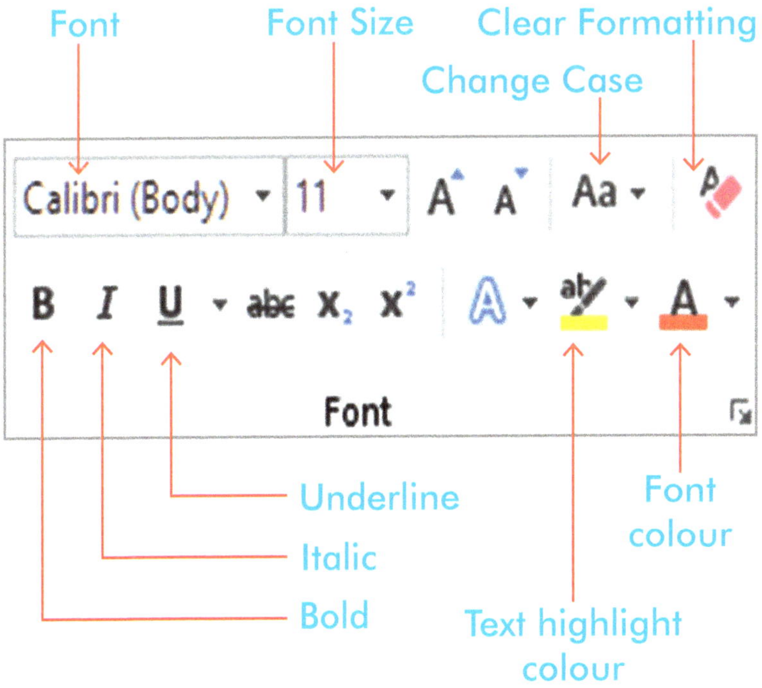

Font
Font Size
Clear Formatting
Change Case
Calibri (Body) 11
Font
Underline
Italic
Bold
Font colour
Text highlight colour

Changing Font of the Text

Font is the look and shape of the letters of the text. There are many fonts available in MS-Word.

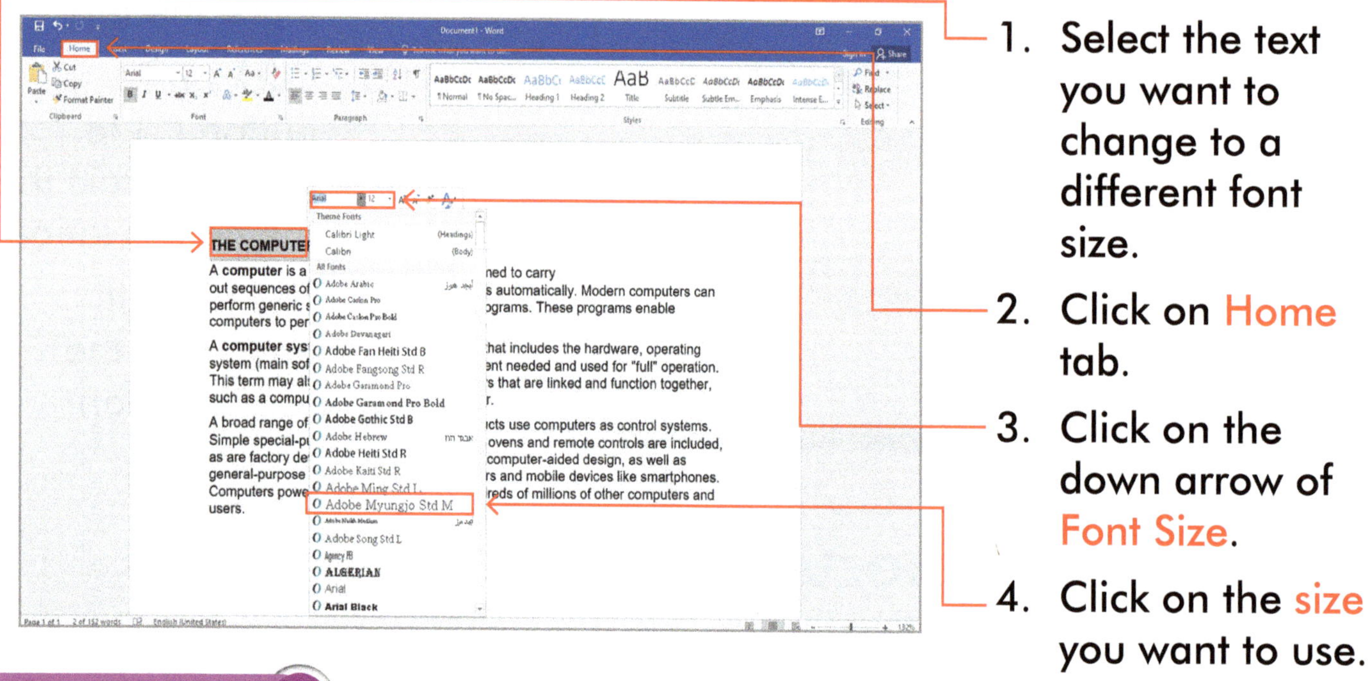

Do you know

A font is a typeface that defines the shape of each character.

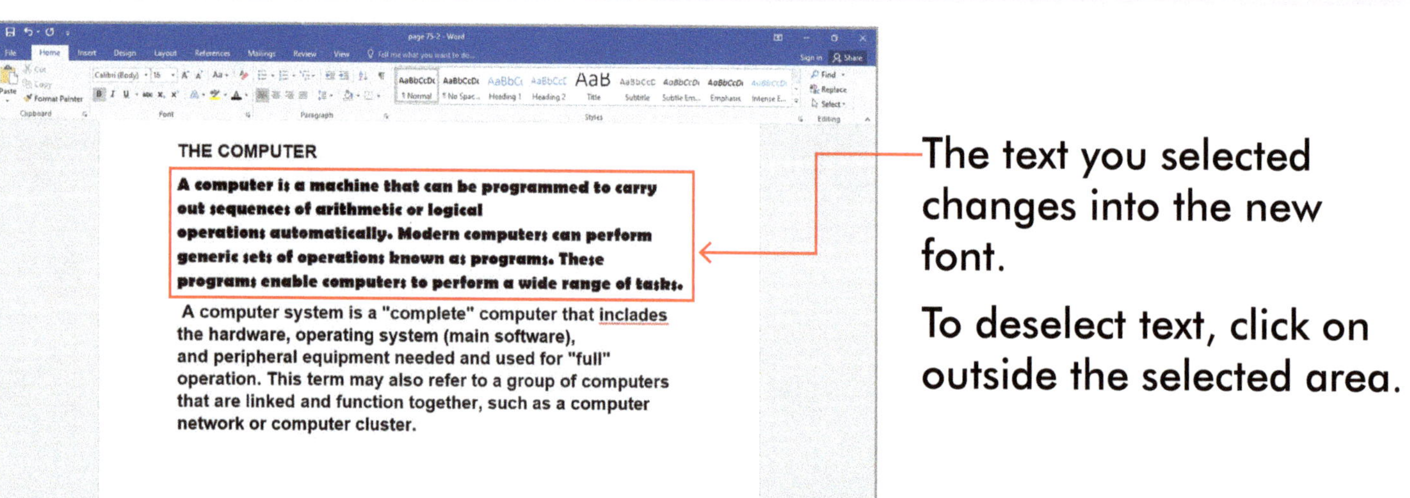

Using Mini Toolbar

A mini toolbar is used to get quick access to common formatting commands. A mini toolbar appears faintly whenever you select any text in the document. Its tools can be activated if you want to use it. If you don't want to use it, you can continue with your working and the toolbar will disappear itself.

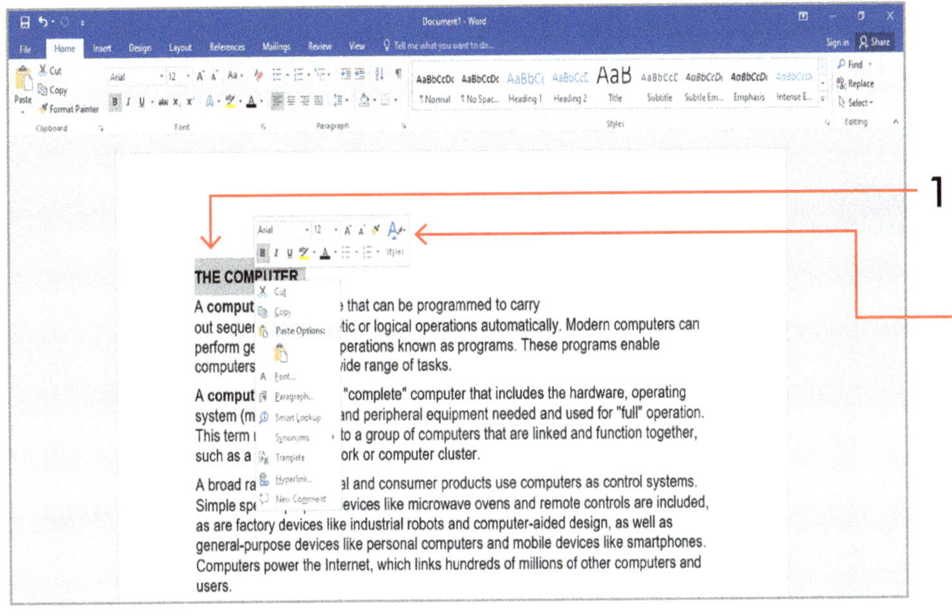

1. Select the text that you want to format.

The mini toolbar appears faintly.

You can also right-click over the selected text to display the toolbar.

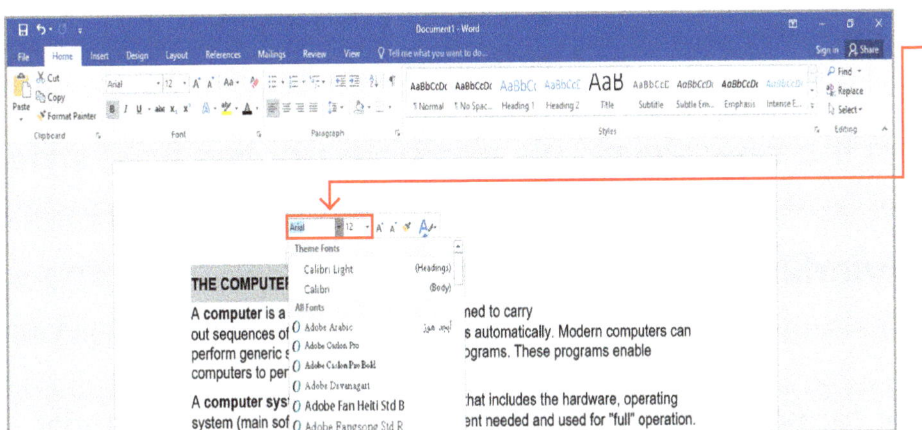

2. Move the mouse pointer over the toolbar and click on the tool (e.g. Font) that you want to activate; then use the tool.

Word immediately applies the formatting.

Changing the Font Size

The size of a letter or character is called font size. You can increase or decrease the font size in your document.

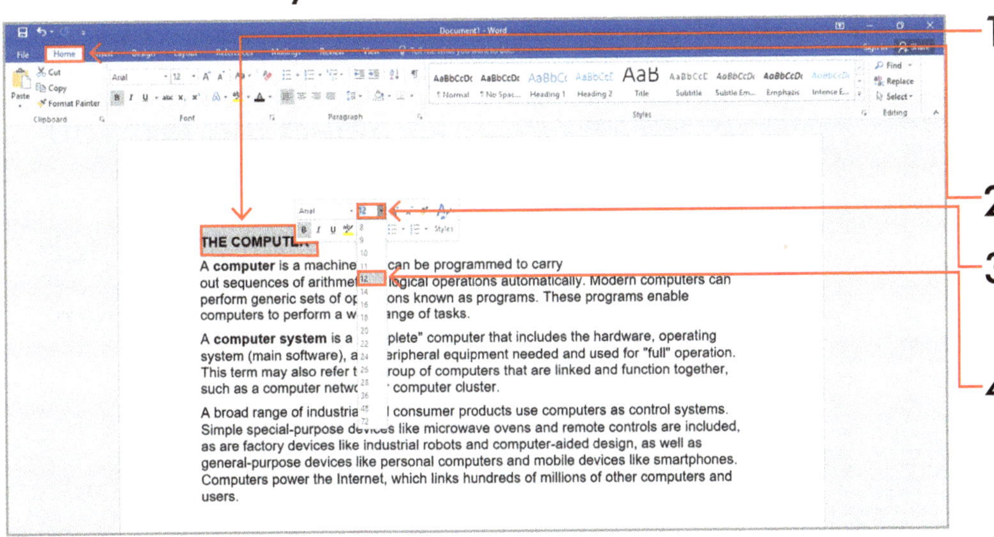

1. Select the text you want to change to a different font size.
2. Click on Home tab.
3. Click on the down arrow of Font Size.
4. Click on the size you want to use.

The text you selected changes into the new size.

Changing the Text Bold, Italic or Underline

You can make your text bold or italic or underline to emphasise information in your document.

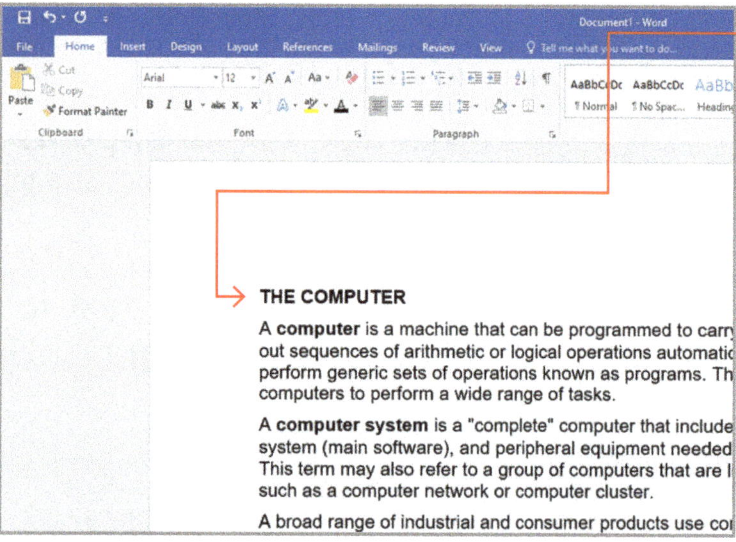

1. Select the text you want to make bold, italicise or underline.
2. Click on Home tab on the ribbon.
3. Click on one of the following buttons:

   (B) Bold (*I*) Italic (U) Underline

The text you selected appears in the new style. This example applies Bold style to the text.

To remove the bold, italic or underline style, repeat steps 1-3.

You can use the keyboard shortcut for bold, italic and underline. Press Ctrl+B to apply bold formatting, Ctrl+I to apply italic, and Ctrl+U to apply underline.

Changing the Colour of Text

The colour of the text can be changed draw attention towards important information in your document or make it attractive.

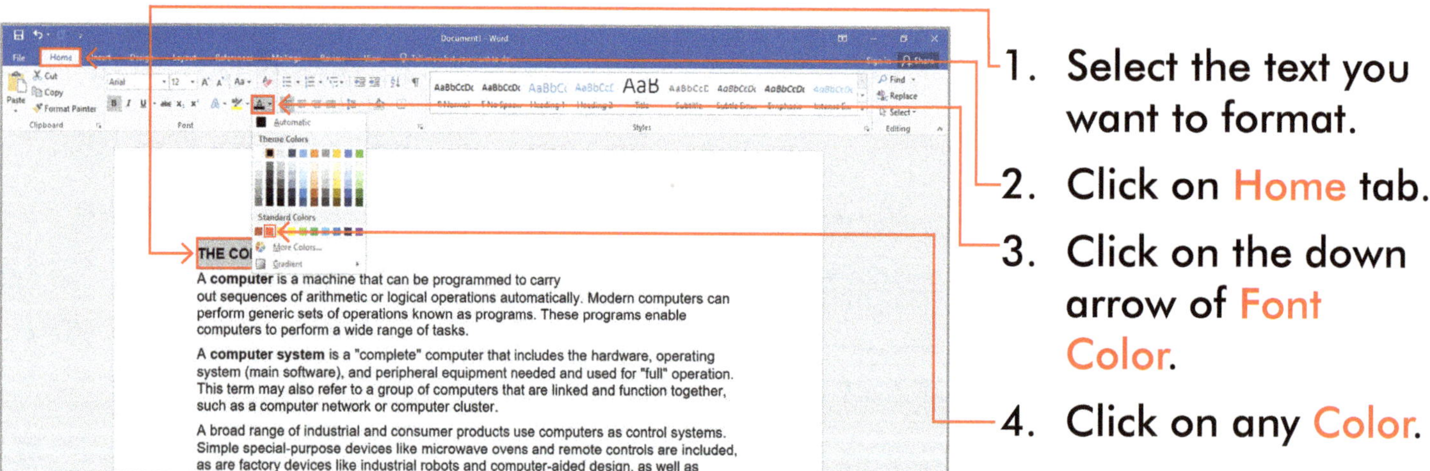

1. Select the text you want to format.
2. Click on Home tab.
3. Click on the down arrow of Font Color.
4. Click on any Color.

Word applies colour to the text. In this example, we apply red colour.

Adding WordArt

You can give your text an artistic look by using the WordArt feature.

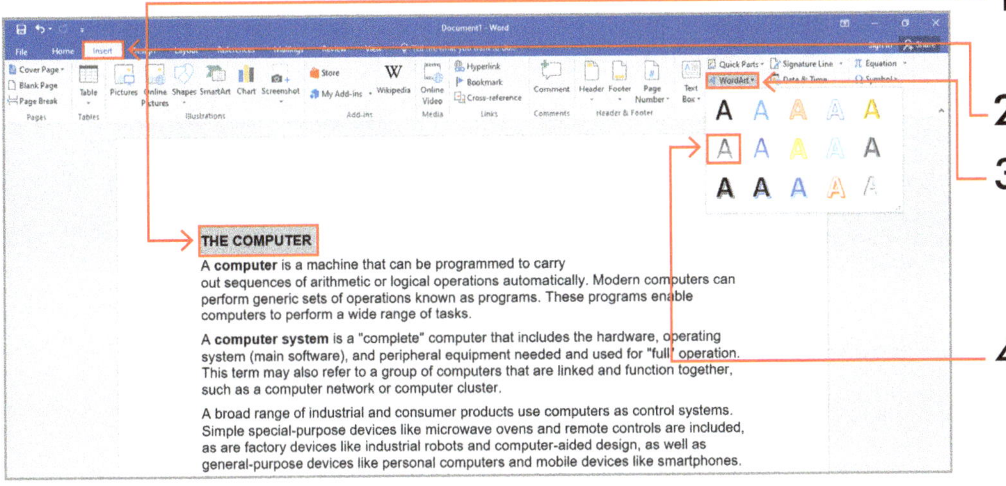

1. Select the text for the WordArt feature.
2. Click on Insert tab.
3. Click on WordArt.

   A list of options will appear.
4. Click on the WordArt style you want to use.

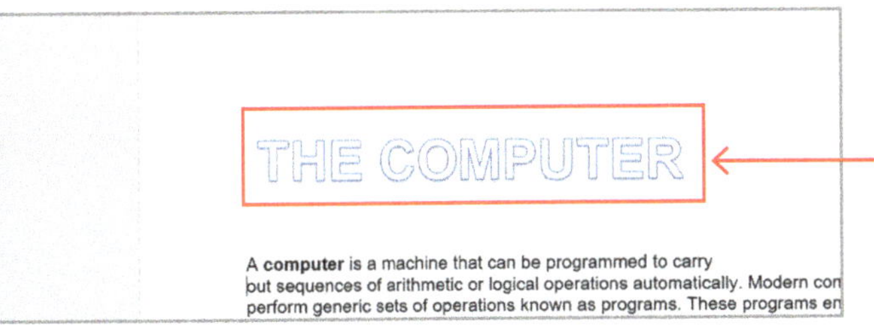

The WordArt appears in a textbox in your document.

5. Click outside the text box to hide the text box.

Changing Alignment of Text

The way in which text is placed in a page is called Alignment. You can align the text as left, centred, right and justified. You can select different alignments according to your requirement. By default, the text is left-aligned.

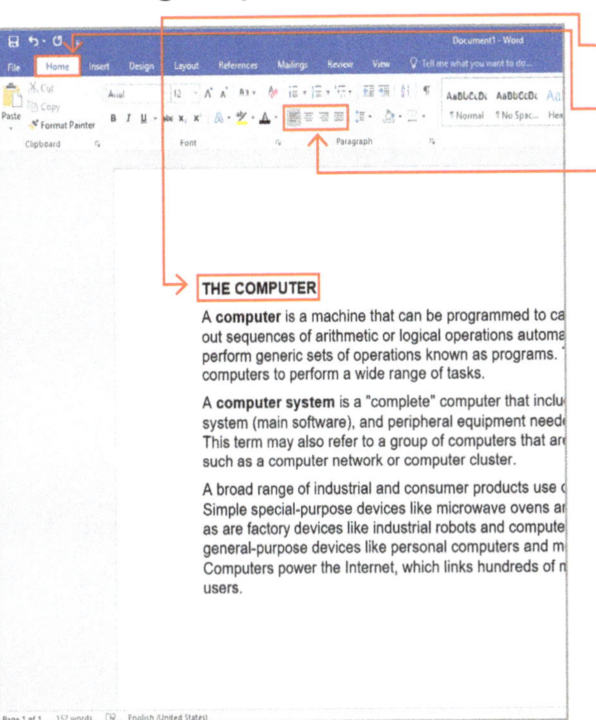

1. Select the text you want to format.
2. Click on Home tab.
3. Click on one of the following buttons :

   ⇒ To left-align text, click on the Align Left (≡) or press Ctrl+L.

   ⇒ To centre the text, click on the Center (≡) or press Ctrl+E.

   ⇒ To right-align text, click on the Align Right (≡) or press Ctrl+R.

   ⇒ To justify text between the left and right margins, click on the Justify (≡) or press Ctrl+J.

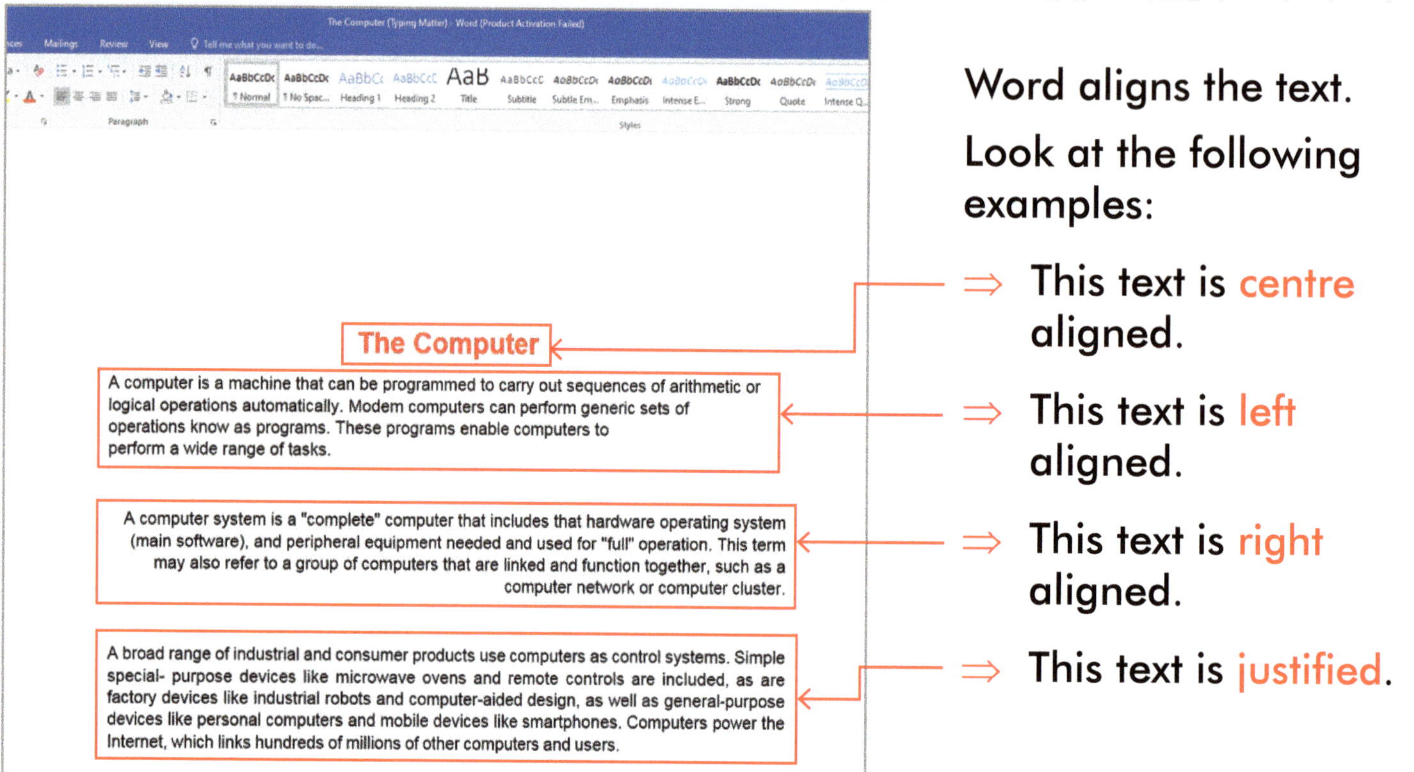

Word aligns the text.

Look at the following examples:

⇒ This text is centre aligned.

⇒ This text is left aligned.

⇒ This text is right aligned.

⇒ This text is justified.

Highlighting the Text

Text can be highlighted for looking different in your document. Highlighting text is useful for marking information you want to review or verify later.

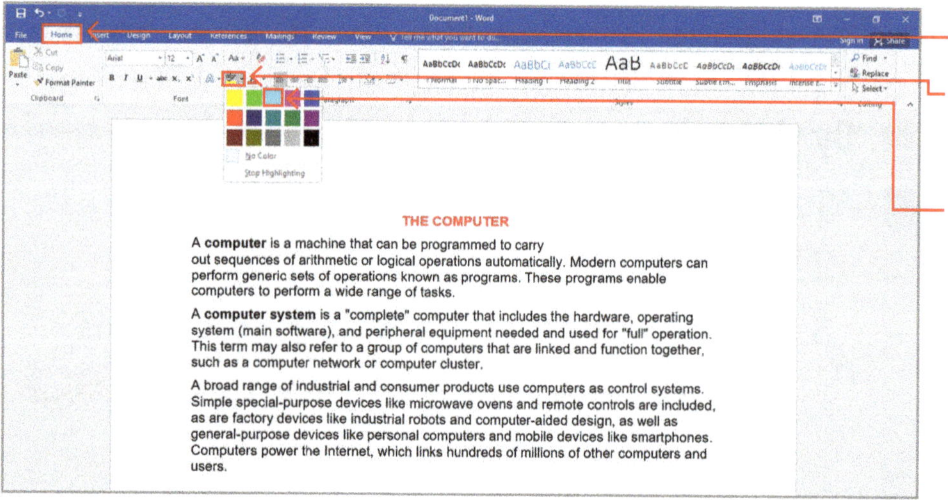

1. Click on Home tab.
2. Click on Text Highlight Color button.
3. Click on a highlight color.

   The mouse pointer changes into (|) when it is over your document.
4. Select each area of text you want to highlight.

   The text you select appears highlighted.
5. When you have finished highlighting the text, press the Esc key from the keyboard.

   To remove highlighting from text, repeat steps 1 to 5, selecting No Color in step 3.

Adding a Border

You can add a border to your document to bring attention to the text.

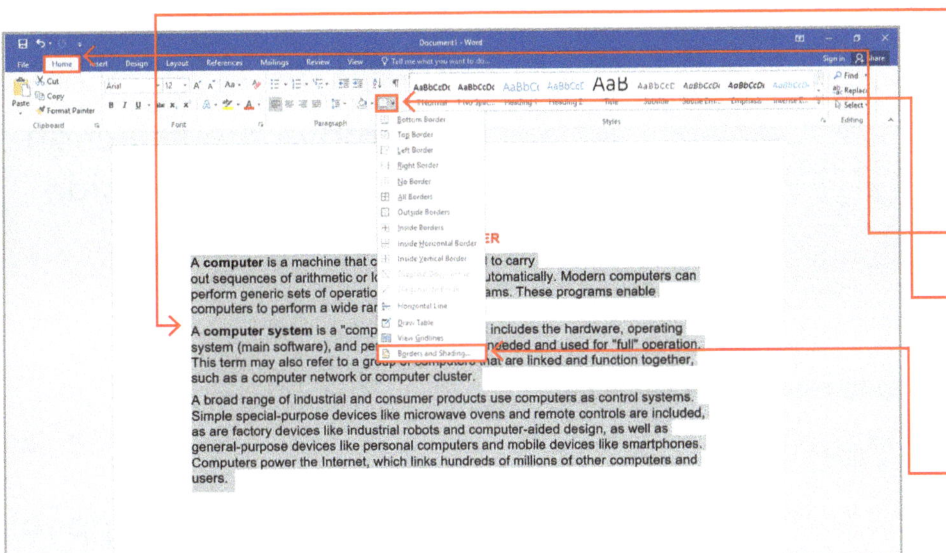

1. Click anywhere in the text or select the text to which you want to add a border.
2. Click on Home tab.
3. Click on the down arrow of Borders button.
4. Click on Borders and Shading.

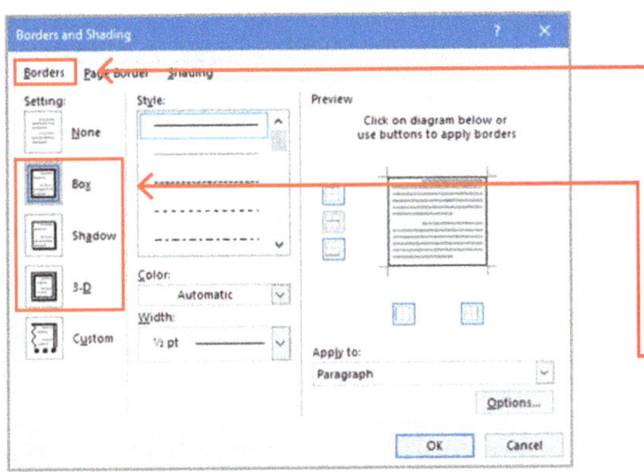

The Borders and Shading dialog box appears.

5. Click on the Borders tab.
6. Click here to select a type of border.
7. Click here to select the style for the border.
8. Click on the down arrow of Colour and select a colour for the border.
9. Click on the down arrow of Width and select a thickness for the border line.

This area shows the preview of the settings you select.

10. Click on OK.

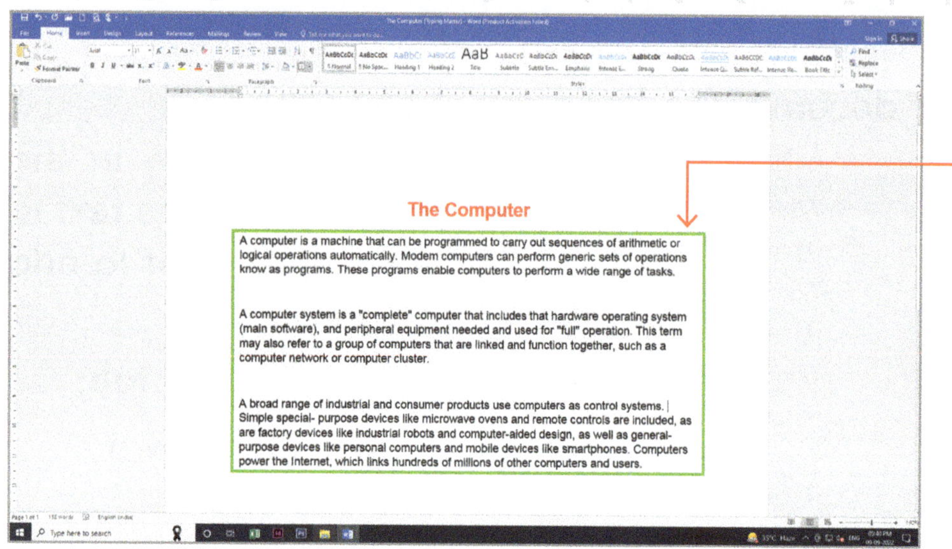

The border appears around the selected text.

To remove the selection click anywhere outside the selection.

Superscript or Subscript Text

You can assign superscript or subscript notation to any text to make it appear above or below the regular line of text. A subscript or superscript is a number, figure, symbol or indicator that appears smaller than the normal line of type and is set slightly below or above it – subscripts appear at or below the baseline, while superscripts are above. Subscripts and superscripts are perhaps best known for their use in formulas and mathematical expressions but have many other uses as well.

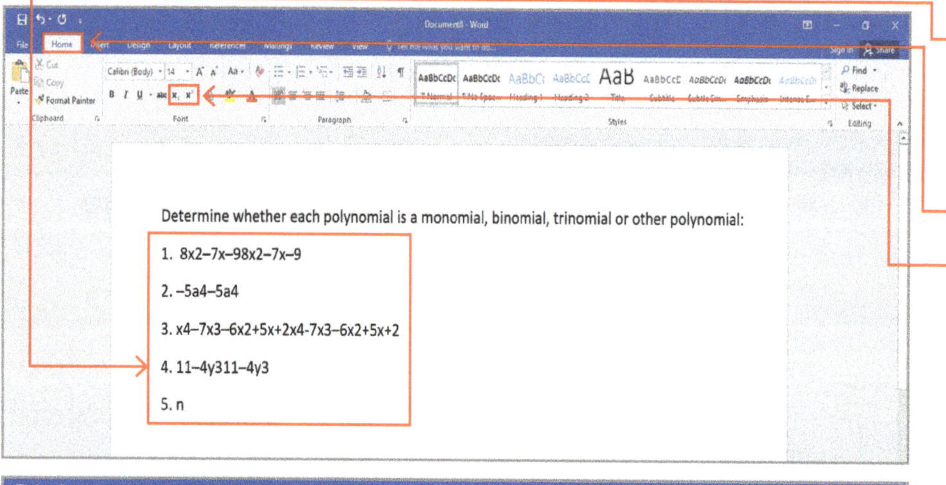

1. Type and select the text that you want to superscript or subscript.
2. Click on the Home tab.
3. Click on the following buttons:

   Superscript button (x^2)

   Subscript button (x_2).

Determine whether each polynomial is a monomial, binomial, trinomial or other polynomial:

1. $8x^2$–7x–$98x^2$–7x–9
2. –5a4–5a4
3. x^4–7x3–6x2+5x+2x4-7x3–$6x^2$+5x+2
4. 11–4y311–$4y^3$
5. n

Word superscripts or subscripts the selected text.

You can click anywhere outside the selection to continue working.

Change Text Case

You can change the case of the text in your document without retyping the text, *i.e.* the text written in small letters can be changed into capital letters or vice versa. Word offers five case styles to choose from.

⇒ **Sentence Case :** The text will be in the form of a sentence, *i.e.* the first character of the sentence will be in capital letters (uppercase) and the rest will be in small letters (lowercase).

⇒ **lowercase :** The text will be changed into small letters by using this option.

⇒ **UPPERCASE :** The text will be changed into capital letters.

⇒ **Capitalize Each Word :** The first character of each word will be capitalised in the text.

⇒ **tOGGLE cASE :** The first character of the word will be small and the rest in uppercase. This option reverses Sentence Case.

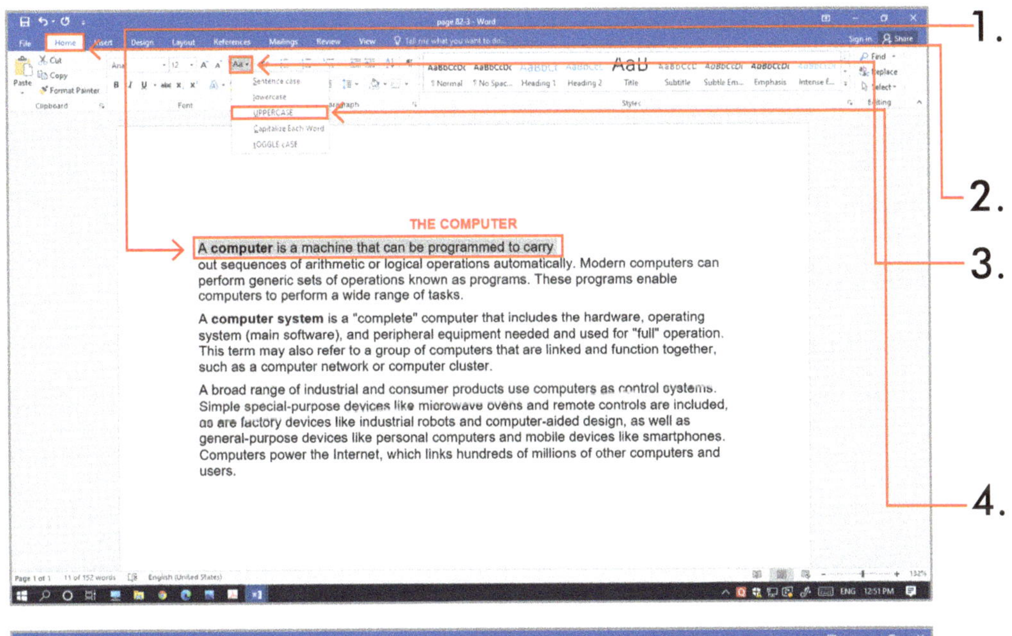

1. Select the text that you want to change to a new case style.
2. Click on Home tab.
3. Click on Change Case button.

   The Change Case menu appears.
4. Click on the case style you want to use.

THE COMPUTER

A COMPUTER IS A MACHINE THAT CAN BE PROGRAMMED TO CARRY out sequences of arithmetic or logical operations automatically. Modern computers can perform generic sets of operations known as programs. These programs enable computers to perform a wide range of tasks.

A computer system is a "complete" computer that includes the hardware, operating system (main software), and peripheral equipment needed and used for "full" operation. This term may also refer to a group of computers that are linked and function together, such as a computer network or computer cluster.

A broad range of industrial and consumer products use computers as control systems. Simple special-purpose devices like microwave ovens and remote controls are included, as are factory devices like industrial robots and computer-aided design, as well as

The text you selected changes into the new case style (Uppercase).

To deselect the text, click on outside the selected area.

LET'S HAVE A LOOK

- You can create a new document in Word any time you want to write a piece of new text.
- MS-Word 2016 is the latest version of Microsoft Word.
- Insertion Point is the point where the next character typed from the keyboard will appear on the screen.
- You can select the whole text or a part of text according to your need.
- Selected text appears highlighted on the screen.
- Moving is to cut the text from the original place and paste it to another place.
- Copying is to copy the text from one place to another.
- Formatting means changing and arranging text in a document to make it attractive.
- All the formatting options can also be used through Font group and Paragraph group in the Home tab.
- Font is the look and shape of the letters of the text.
- The way in which text is placed in page is called Alignment.

BRAIN TEASER

1. Answer the following questions:

a. What is the use of creating a new document?

____

____

b. What is formatting?

____

____

c. Write the different methods of selecting the text.

____

____

d. What is mini toolbar?

____

____

2. Answer each of the following in one word or line:

a. What is Insertion Point?

____

b. Name any two fonts used in MS-Word.

____

c. Name the four types of alignments.

____

d. Name the feature that gives text tool in artistic tool.

____

3. Write the shortcut keys to:

a. Save text _______________

b. Make something bold _______________

c. Italicize _______________

d. Underline _______________

e. Left align _______________

f. Right align _______________

g. Centre align _______________

h. Justify _______________

4. Fill in the blanks:

a. You can enter text into a document with the help of _______________.

b. A _______________ is a typeface that defines the shape of each character.

c. Selected text appears _______________ on the screen.

d. _______________ is a feature through which you can write any text in artistic way.

e. By default, Word assigns the _______________ align.

f. To select a single word, _______________ on the Word.

g. _______________ command is used to make a duplicate copy of text.

5. Multiple Choice Questions

Tick (✓) the correct answer:

a. The point where the next character typed from the keyboard will appear

i. Pointer ☐ ii. Insertion point ☐ iii. Arrow ☐

b. You can insert the text with the help of a

i. Mouse ☐ ii. Pencil ☐ iii. Keyboard ☐

c. Changing and arranging text in a document to make it attractive

i. Editing ☐ ii. Formatting ☐ iii. Writing ☐

d. The shortcut key to save a document is

i. Shift+S ☐ ii. Ctrl+S ☐ iii. Ctrl+A ☐

e. The shortcut key to make the text bold

i. Ctrl+R ☐ ii. Ctrl+S ☐ iii. Ctrl+B ☐

f. The shortcut key to right-align the text

i. Alt+O ☐ ii. Shift+O ☐ iii. Ctrl+R ☐

Open MS-Word, type the following text and create a document.

UNITY

There is a saying : "United we stand, divided we fall." A single hand has a limited capacity, but more hands working together will have much more strength to apply on a particular thing at the same time. So, we should be united in all our missions of life.

In case of a country, when the native land is attacked by any outside enemy, it is not a single person's or a few persons' job to fight against the enemy. It is the collective force of all the countrymen to fight out the evil.

This unity is always proved to be a great source of strength. It is really like an invincible constructive performance.

- Format it as it is shown above.
- Save the document by your name.
- Select the heading and delete it.
- Now add the heading by using WordArt.
- Add a page border to it.
- Close the document and exit from the Word.

Formative Assessment-3
(Chapters 5-7)

1. In the wordsearch given below the components of Word window are hidden. Find them out.

P	R	N	G	K	T	Z	Y	C	T	L	C	P	G
Q	S	T	A	T	U	S	B	A	R	M	O	N	T
C	T	S	C	R	O	C	L	B	A	R	N	R	G
B	K	L	R	T	R	C	T	S	T	N	T	C	L
G	A	H	F	I	L	E	T	A	B	D	R	X	V
Y	R	S	B	Q	N	E	L	M	Z	W	O	Y	N
G	O	Q	M	S	R	C	G	A	D	G	E	T	S
R	F	B	D	G	L	K	B	J	B	C	L	A	R
N	Q	E	R	T	F	N	Q	F	R	S	B	C	L
I	N	S	E	R	T	I	O	N	P	O	I	N	T
Q	A	E	R	O	P	E	E	K	G	P	L	C	N
F	P	C	T	L	S	U	X	Z	V	N	C	O	R

2. Write the name of alignment (left, centre, right and justify) for each of the following paragraphs:

All flowers have four basic parts: sepals, petals, carpels and stamens. Different flowers have different numbers and shapes of these parts.	All flowers have four basic parts: sepals, petals, carpels and stamen. Different flowers have different numbers and shapes of these parts.	All flowers have four basic parts: sepals, petals, carpels and stamen. Different flowers have different numbers and shapes of these parts.	All flowers have four basic parts: sepals, petals, carpels and stamen. Different flowers have different numbers and shapes of these parts.
____________	____________	____________	____________

3. Label the following:

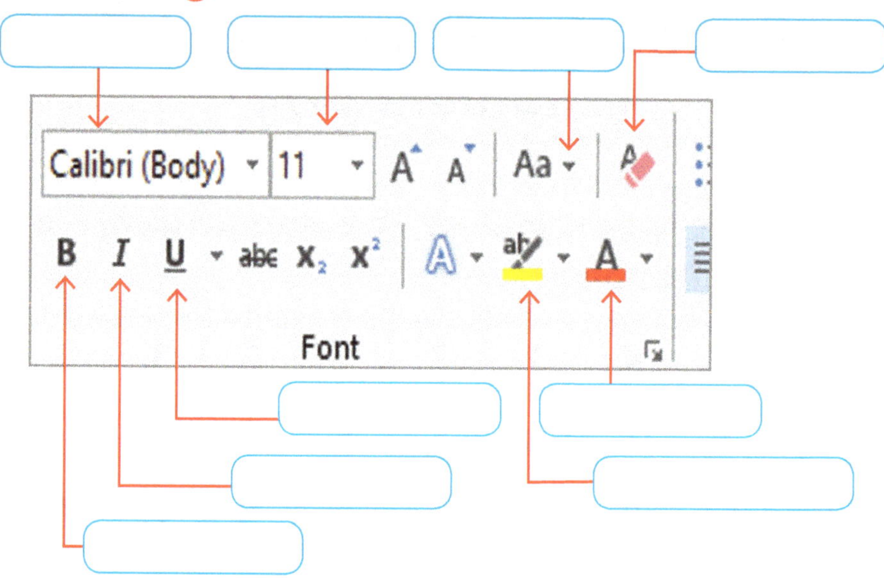

4. Answer the following questions:

a. How can you personalise a desktop?

b. Write the different picture options of the image on a screen.

c. What is Microsoft Word?

d. What is formatting?

e. What is Backstage view?

8 More Commands In LOGO

Dear children, you studied about LOGO and its commands in the previous class. Now let's move ahead and learn some more interesting commands of LOGO.

LOGO

LOGO is a programming language. LOGO stands for 'Language of Graphics Oriented.' It is used to draw different shapes and figures using the keyboard.

LOGO uses the turtle, which looks like a triangle, to draw figures and lines on the screen. The turtle can move right, left, backward and forward after getting our commands or instructions. When the turtle moves, it draws a line behind it.

Before moving ahead let's first revise the commands you previously came across.

Home	This command is used to bring the turtle to the centre of the main screen from any position by leaving the line behind.
Forward (FD)	This command draws a line by moving the turtle in forward direction by giving the number of steps.
Backward (BK)	This command brings the turtle in the backward direction by giving the number of steps.
Right (RT)	This command is used to turn the turtle to the right side in the clock-wise direction by giving the number of turns.
Left (LT)	This command is used to turn the turtle to the left side in the anti-clockwise direction by giving the number of turns.
Hideturtle (HT)	This command is used to hide the turtle so that it may disappear from the screen.

Showturtle (ST) This command is used to show the hidden turtle again on the screen.

Penup (PU) This command is used to lift the turtle's penup and let it move without drawing any line on the screen.

Pendown (PD) This command will again lift the turtle's pendown and start drawing again on the screen.

Clearscreen (CS) This command is used to clear the drawing area of the screen and bring the turtle back home.

COLOURS IN LOGO

You can colour the screen by filling the colours in drawing. You can change the colour of LOGO Turtle (pen) by using some particular LOGO commands.

There are 15 predefined colours of LOGO wherein each number has a colour defined. The colour can be used by just giving the number which corresponds to that colour. All the primary colours in computer (Red, Green, Blue) have 256 different shades, each of which after mixing brings out the result.

Colour Number	Colour Code	Colour
0.	[0 0 0]	Black
1.	[0 0 255]	Blue
2.	[0 255 0]	Green
3.	[0 255 255]	Cyan
4.	[255 0 0]	Red
5.	[255 0 255]	Magenta
6.	[255 255 0]	Yellow
7.	[255 255 255]	White
8.	[155 96 59]	Brown
9.	[197 136 18]	Light Brown
10.	[100 162 64]	Dark Green
11.	[120 187 187]	Darkish Blue
12.	[255 149 119]	Tan
13.	[144 113 208]	Violet
14.	[255 163 0]	Orange
15.	[183 183 183]	Grey

Do you know ?

You can also change the colour of the lines, screen and flood (filling) in LOGO.

The width or the size of the line can be changed by using SET commands.

Set Screen Colour

The function of the SETSCREENCOLOR is to set the colour of drawing area by the specified colour. We can type the colour number in front of the primitive.

SETSCREENCOLOR 4

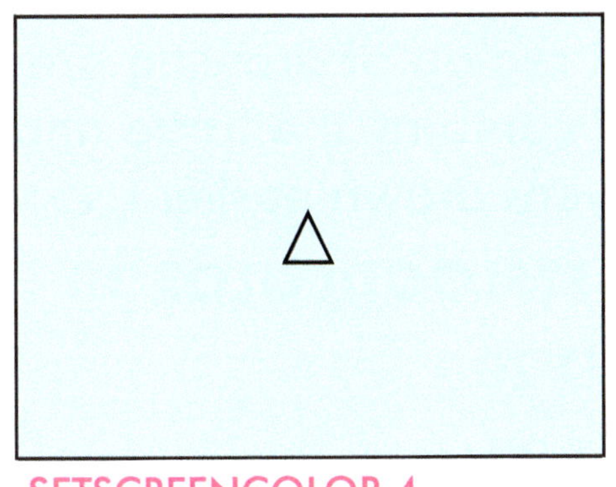

SETSCREENCOLOR 4

Set Pen Colour

The pen colour of Logo is by default black. If we want to change the pen colour, we can use SETPENCOLOR command.

The colour of pen will be changed by SETPENCOLOR, with the help of colour number.

SETSCREENCOLOR 7

FD 20

RT 90

FD 50

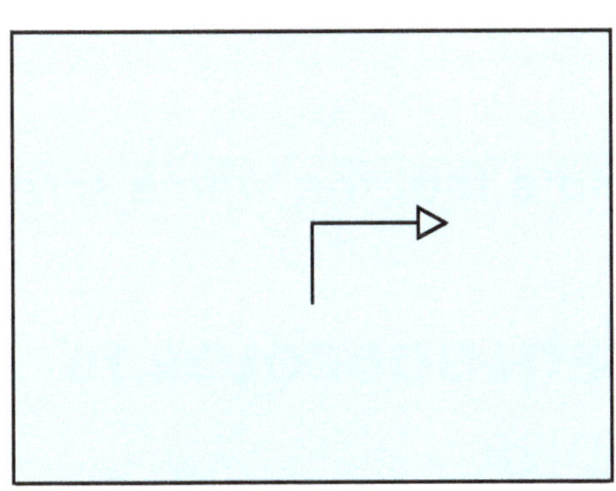

SETSCREENCOLOR 4
SETPENCOLOR 7
FD 20
RT 90
FD 50

The text in SETPENCOLOR is also written with the coloured pen.

LABEL "Pencolor"

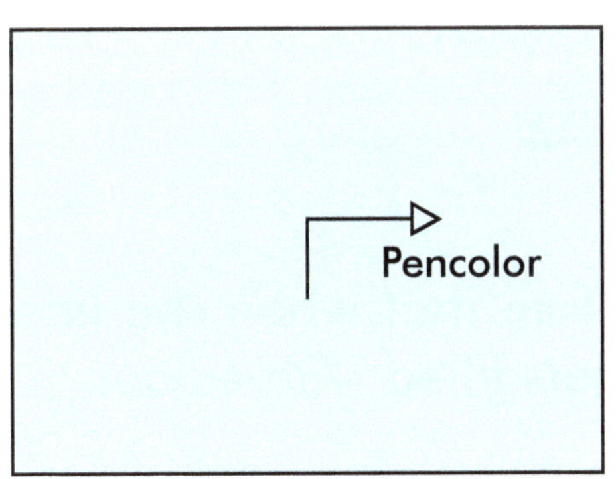

SETSCREENCOLOR 4
SETPENCOLOR 7
FD 20
RT 90
FD 50
LABEL "Pencolor"

Set Flood Colour

If we want to colour an enclosed figure, we may use SETFLOODCOLOR command.

Here, the particular colour is set, with which different shapes can be filled in.

SETFLOODCOLOR 10

Fill

A region of drawing area filled in by Fill command. It contains the turtle and is bounded by lines which were drawn earlier.

SETFLOODCOLOR 10

FD 20

RT 90

FD 50

FILL

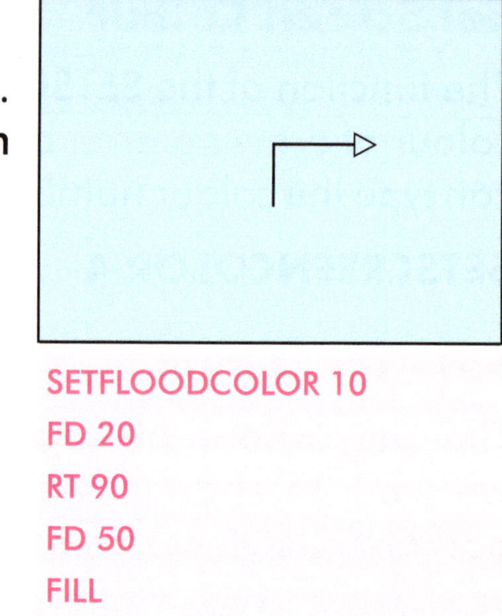

SETFLOODCOLOR 10
FD 20
RT 90
FD 50
FILL

Note that the whole screen will fill if the lines do not close.

SETFLOODCOLOR 10

FD 20

RT 90

FD 50

RT 90

FD 20

RT 90

FD 50

FILL

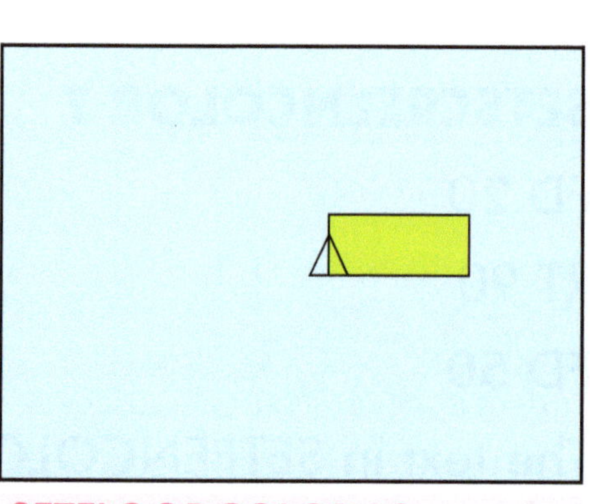

SETFLOODCOLOR 10
FD 20
RT 90
FD 50
RT 90
FD 20
RT 90
FD 50
FILL

Note that when the lines are close then the figure gets filled with colour.

REPEAT COMMAND

Writing work in text area is reduced when the same command is repeated for a specified number of times.

The REPEAT command reduces the number of the lines of commands you need to write in order to draw.

For example: look at the following commands. They can draw a square.

FD 100

RT 90

FD 100

RT 90

FD 100

RT 90

FD 100

RT 90

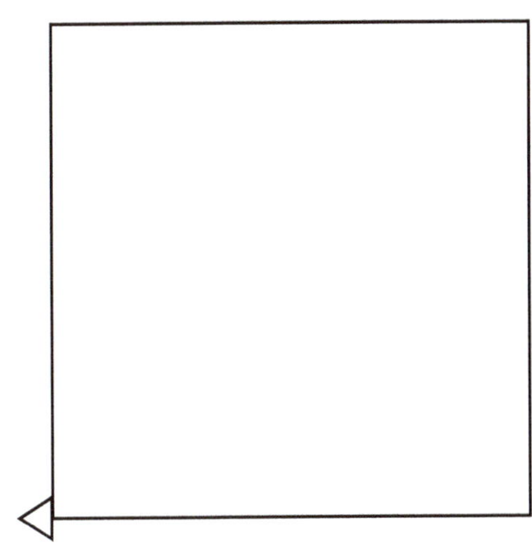

After typing the above set of commands, you will get a square.

But, did you notice that the set of commands FD 100 and RT 90 in the above example is repeated four times?

Therefore, there is no need for writing the same commands four times. We can use REPEAT command to draw the square.

REPEAT <space> <Number of times> <space> [Command to be repeated]

Using the REPEAT command, the command to draw a square, therefore, becomes

REPEAT 4 [FD 100 RT 90]

In the above example, the FD 100 RT 90 is repeated 4 times as there are 4 turns in a square.

Similarly, you can draw a polygon like a triangle, pentagon, hexagon, septagon and an octagon. When you make any shape, the turtle has to walk around the edges and turn through 360 degrees before coming back home.

To understand how much turn a turtle will take to complete the shape of a triangle, let's take an example.

The turtle makes x turns for a triangle with x-sides; the side of each turn will be 360/x degrees. So, the triangle has 3 sides and it will turn 120 degrees (360/3).

Turtle makes 3 sides and takes the turn of 120° to make a triangle.

Turtle makes 4 sides and takes the turn of 90° to make a square.

Turtle makes 5 sides and takes the turn of 72° to make a pentagon.

Turtle makes 6 sides and takes the turn of 60° to make a hexagon.

Turtle makes 7 sides and takes the turn of 51° to make a septagon.

Turtle makes 8 sides and takes the turns of 45° to make an octagon.

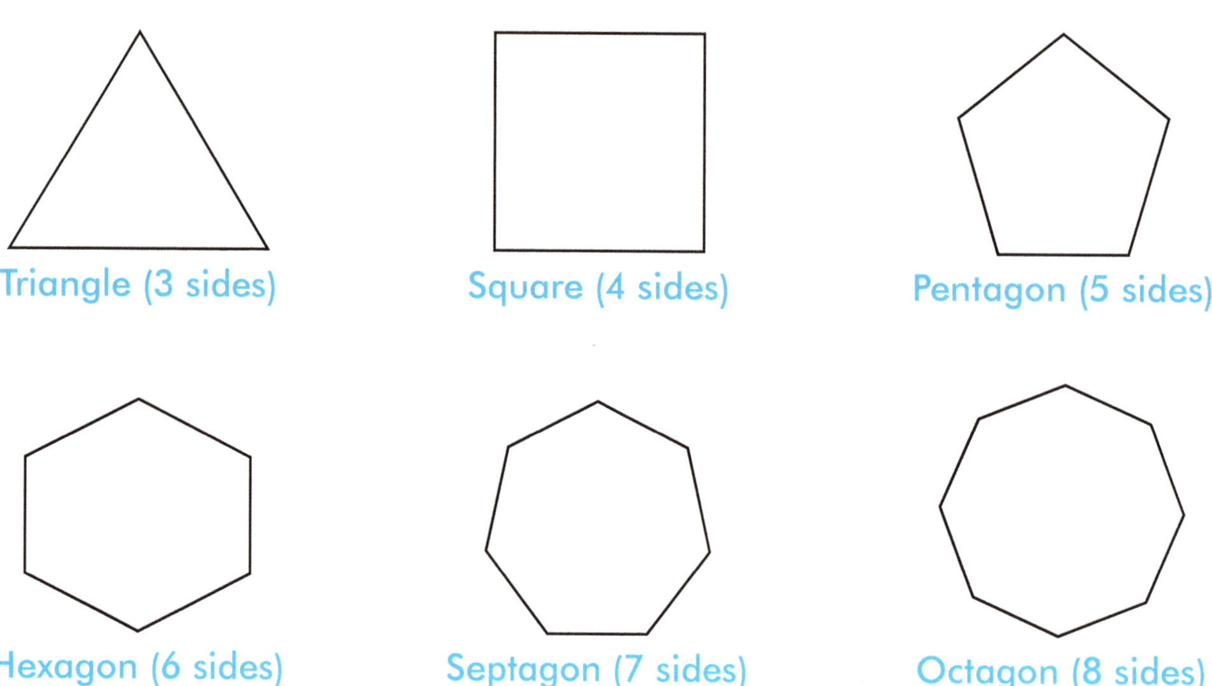

Triangle

In a triangle, there are three sides. Therefore, the turtle will turn 120 degrees, *i.e.* (360/3). So, the command will be written as:

REPEAT 3 [FD 100 RT 120]

Similarly, you can draw another shape of a polygon.

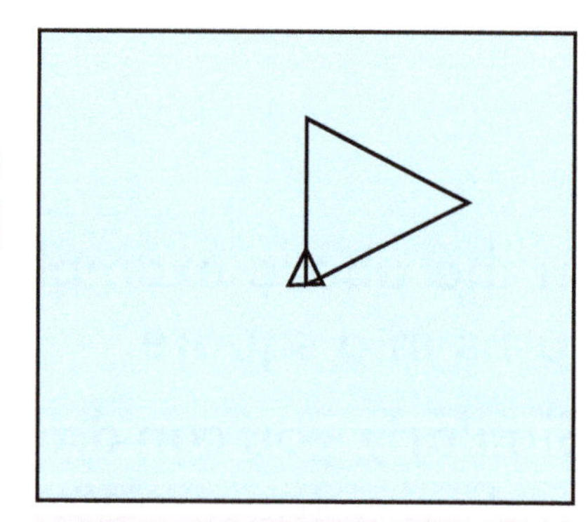

REPEAT 3 [FD 100 RT 120]

Drawing Circles or Curves Using Repeat Command

You can also draw circles, semi-circles and curves by using REPEAT command.

RT 1 will turn the turtle slightly (just by one turn) to the right. Typing FD 1 after this will move the turtle forward by one turtle unit.

A full circle is drawn with 360° and a semi-circle with 180°.

If you repeat the command 360 times with the following command set :

REPEAT 360 [FD 1 RT 1]

you will get a complete circle.

If you repeat the command 180 times with the following command set :

REPEAT 360 [FD 1 RT 1] — Complete circle

REPEAT 180 [FD 1 RT 1] — Half circle

REPEAT 180 [FD 1 RT 1]

you will get a half circle.

The size of a circle can be changed by changing the number with FD and RT commands.

In the following ways a circle of different sizes can be drawn:

Repeat 72 [FD 5 RT 5]

Repeat 36 [FD 5 RT 10]

Repeat 18 [FD 10 RT 20] and so on.

It reflects that the command should be repeated 360/N times where N is the angle turned by the turtle, *i.e.* RT N.

Repeat 360/N [FD X RT N]

PRINT COMMAND

You can use PRINT Command to display anything on the LOGO screen. The message to be written should be closed in quotes " " or square brackets [ ].

Syntax : **PRINT [Text]**

Or

PR [Text]

For example : **PRINT [A Computer is an electronic device.]**

It will print the message : **A Computer is an electronic device.**

PRINT command is also used to perform mathematical operations, like Addition (+), Subtraction (-), Multiplication (*) and Division (/). The mathematical operations are not enclosed in quotes " " or square brackets [ ]. If they are enclosed in quotes or brackets, it is treated as a message.

For example :

To add any two numbers:

PRINT 40+30

70

To subtract any two numbers:

PRINT 50–10

40

To multiply any two numbers:

PRINT 12*5

60

To divide any two numbers:

PRINT 100/4

25

LET'S HAVE A LOOK

- With SETSCREENCOLOR the colour of the screen changes.
- With SETPENCOLOR the pen colour changes.
- With SETFLOODCOLOR the fill colour is set.
- The area set with SETFLOODCOLOR is filled with fill, containing the turtle.
- The same instructions are repeated a number of times by the repeat command.
- PRINT Command is used to display anything on the LOGO screen.

BRAIN TEASER

1. Answer the following questions:

a. What is the use of LOGO?

b. What is the use of REPEAT command?

c. Which command will you use to fill colour in an enclosed shape?

d. Differentiate between SETSCREENCOLOR and SETPENCOLOR command.

e. How can we draw a circle in LOGO using the REPEAT command?

f. How many polygons can you draw using REPEAT command? Name them.

2. Write the commands to draw the following objects:

a. Square ____________________

b. Hexagon ____________________

c. Pentagon ____________________

d. Circle ____________________

e. Semi-circle ____________________

f. Triangle ____________________

g. Fill the screen with red colour ____________________

3. Write the full forms of the following:

a. FD ____________________

b. BK ____________________

c. RT ____________________

d. LT ____________________

e. CS ____________________

f. PU ____________________

g. PD ____________________

4. Fill in the blanks:

a. ____________ is the colour code of dark green.

b. To change the screen colour use ____________ command.

c. ____________ changes the colour of a Logo pen.

d. ____________ command changes the background colour of text area.

e. SETPENCOLOR 7 command will change the colour to ____________.

5. Write '**T**' for true and '**F**' for false in the boxes:

a. You can draw polygons easily using REPEAT commands. ☐

b. SETFLOODCOLOR sets the fill colour. ☐

c. LOGO has 16 predefined colours. ☐

d. Using LOGO's coloured pen you can write text in various colours. ☐

e. SETSCREENCOLOR changes the background of your drawing. ☐

6. Multiple Choice Questions:

Tick (✓) the correct answer:

a. The command used to take the turtle to the centre of the screen

i. Home ☐ ii. Center ☐ iii. Repeat ☐

b. The command used to draw a circle

i. Circle ☐ ii. Repeat ☐ iii. Print ☐

c. Which command is used to change pen colour in LOGO?

i. Repeat ☐ ii. SETPENCOLOR ☐

iii. Fill ☐

d. The triangle-shaped object in LOGO screen

i. Square ☐ ii. Turtle ☐ iii. Mouse ☐

e. To draw an octagon, the degree of turn will be

i. 45° ☐ ii. 55° ☐ iii. 40° ☐

f. Which command is used to draw a triangle

i. REPEAT 3 [FD 100 RT 120] ☐

ii. REPEAT 5 [FD 100 RT 120] ☐

iii. REPEAT 3 [FD 150 RT 180] ☐

LAB ACTIVITY

1. Draw the following shapes by using Repeat command:

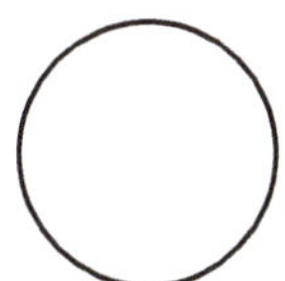

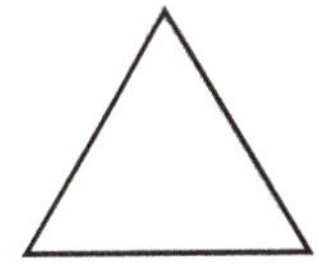
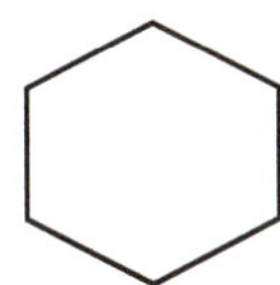

2. Write the LOGO command to solve the following:

a. To find the sum of the first five odd numbers [1+3+5+7+9]

b. To find the multiplication of [15*4]

c. To display the message "I Love My Country."

d. Find the difference between 55 and 33.

9 The Internet

Dear children, you must be knowing that today is the world of the Internet and it has become the biggest and easiest means of communication and gaining knowledge today. So, knowledge about the computer without the knowledge of the Internet is incomplete. Now, let's have some knowledge of the Internet as well.

INTERNET

The Internet is a worldwide system of computer networks in which millions of computers are connected. It can be described as a network of networks. In fact, the Internet is a collection of "interconnected networks". Using the Internet, data can be rapidly transferred around the world. Any type of information or person can be searched for on this network.

However, just because nobody owns the Internet, that doesn't mean it is not monitored and maintained in different ways. The Internet Society, a non-profit organization, established in 1992, oversees the formation of the policies and protocols (rules) that define how we interact by means of the Internet.

Computer network all over the world

INTERNET

USES OF INTERNET

The Internet can be used for various purposes, such as:

Providing Information

The Internet is a large warehouse of information. You can get any type of information at any time sitting at one place.

Communicating

Today, the Internet is the biggest means of communication. You can communicate with any person sitting in any corner of the world in just a second.

E-mail is the example of communicating.

Video Conferencing

Using a Web camera and the software in your computer, you can conduct a meeting face to face even if the other person is in the other corner of the world. It works like a two-way TV-set with real-time audio and video.

Buying and Selling

E-commerce—the online buying and selling of goods and services—is a big part of the Internet. On the Internet, anybody can now buy and sell things while sitting at home.

That saves one's time and money too.

Chatting

Chatting allows you to exchange the typed messages with another person on the Internet. A message you send will instantly appear on the other person's computer.

Sending E-Greetings Cards

You can send greetings cards to your friends through the Internet. The greetings cards on the Internet are referred to as E-greetings cards.

Music on Internet

You can listen to old movie songs, albums, latest movie songs, pop, bhangra, ghazals or remixes on the Internet.

Games

You can play online games, like chess, snookers, puzzles, car race, etc. on the Internet.

Advertisement

Many companies make their websites on the Internet to advertise their products.

Watch Media on Web

You can use the Internet to play digital media, including video files, animations and movies. You can either copy or purchase the media and store it on your computer, or you can play media directly from a website. YouTube is a video sharing platform that is one of the most popular sites on the Web.

REQUIREMENTS FOR AN INTERNET CONNECTION

For an Internet connection, you need the following things:

Computer

For an Internet connection, you need a computer with all the features like speed processor, enough memory, speakers, microphone, etc.

Modem

It is a device that is used to connect a computer with a telephone line in order to get connected to the Internet. The speed of a modem is measured in kbps (Kilobytes Per Second). Modem is an acronym for Modulator/Demodulator.

Telephone Line

Information is carried through one computer to another through telephone lines. The telephone cable is connected to the computer through a modem.

Internet Service Provider (ISP)

The ISP provides a connection to the Internet and allows you to access to the Internet. Airtel, AT&T Internet, Xfinity Internet, Spectrum Internet, Jio, etc., are some of the most popular ISP's.

Software

To search for the information from different Websites, a software called Web Browser is required.

A Web browser provides all the information regarding text, video, animation, etc., present in the Website. Some popular Web browsers are: Google Chrome, Microsoft Edge, Safari, etc.

TERMS RELATED TO INTERNET

Here are some of the terms that you will come across while working on the Internet.

World Wide Web (WWW)

World Wide Web is a widely used information system on the Internet that provides information in the form of text, animation, pictures and videos. World Wide Web was developed by Tim Berners-Lee, in 1989.

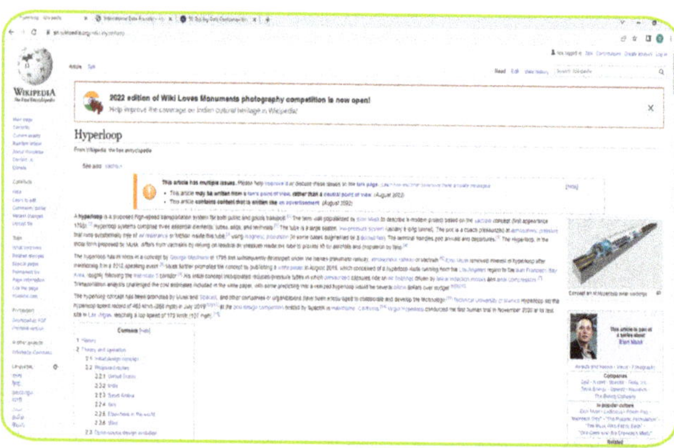

Web Page

Web page is a single page on the internet that contains information in the form of text, graphics, sound or video.

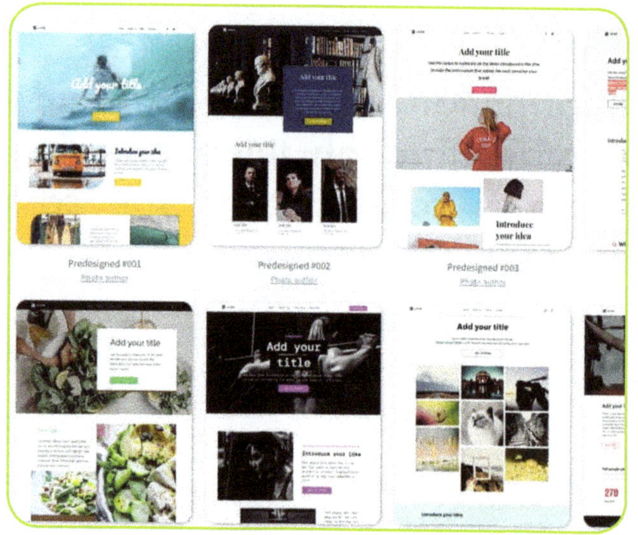

Website

A Website is a set of interconnected web pages. It provides information about many things, such as persons, educational institutes and games.

Home Page

The first page which appears, when we open a Website, is called home page.

For example, look at the home page of www.tesla.com.

This page contains the introduction to the Website.

Hyperlink

A Web page consists of many things besides text and pictures. It also contains hyperlinks which are highlighted text or images that are on the Web pages.

A hyperlink text underlines and is shown in different colours. Hyperlinks lead to the part of the Web page to which they are linked. On moving the mouse pointer over a hyperlink, the mouse pointer simply takes the shape of a hand.

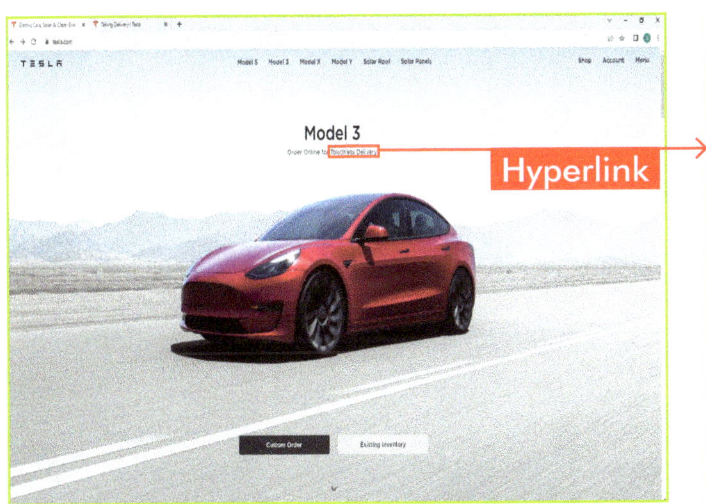

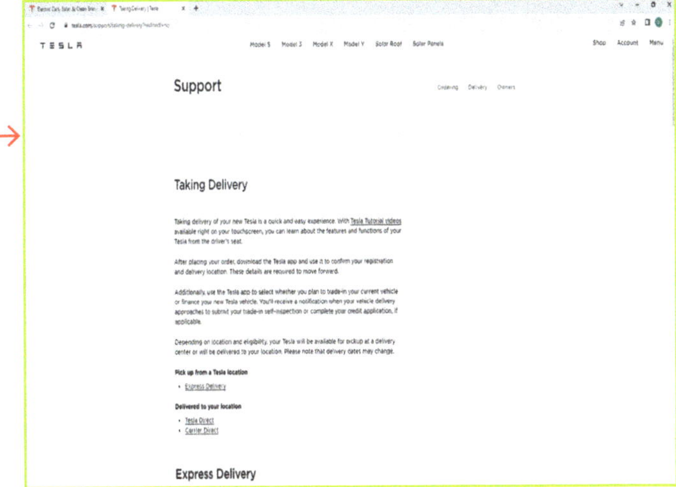

Uniform Resource Locator (URL)

Every Website on the Internet has a unique address. The address of a website or Web page is called the Uniform Resource Locator or URL.

A Web page URL starts with http (Hypertext Transfer Protocol) and contains the computer name, directory name and name of the Web page.

For example, the URL for Tesla Website is:

http://www.tesla.com

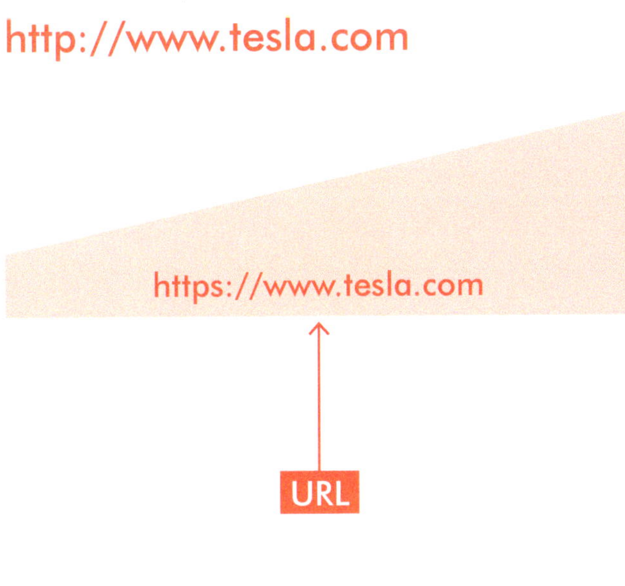

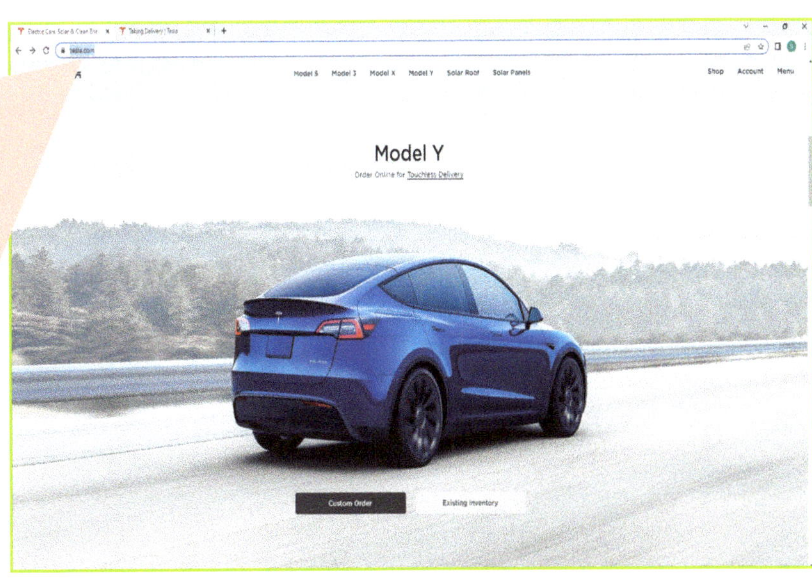

LET'S HAVE A LOOK

- The Internet is a world-wide system of computers.
- We need a computer, a modem, a telephone line, an ISP connection and a Web browser to get connected to the Internet.
- World Wide Web (www) is a widely used information system on the Internet.
- A Website is a set of interconnected Web pages.
- A Web page is a single page on the internet that contains information in the form of text, graphics, sound or video.
- Home page is the first page that appears, when we open a Website.
- The address of a Web page or Website is called URL.

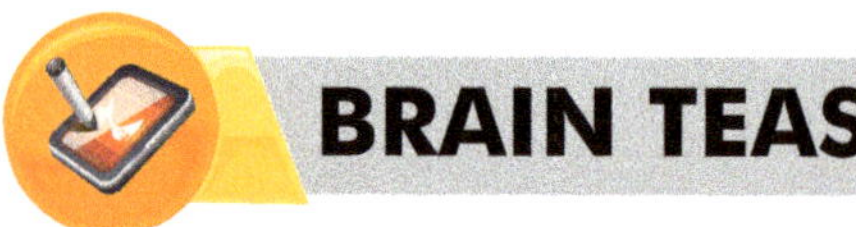

BRAIN TEASER

1. Answer the following questions:

a. What is the Internet?

b. Explain the use of the Internet?

c. What are the requirements to get connected to the Internet?

d. What is a Modem?

2. Define the following:

a. WWW

b. Website

c. Web Page

d. Hyperlink

e. URL

3. Multiple Choice Questions

Tick (✓) the correct answer:

a. Which of these is not a Web browser?
   i. Google Chrome ☐
   ii. Modem ☐
   iii. Safari ☐

b. Hyperlink pointer looks like
   i. ☐ ii. ☐ iii. ☐

c. A famous ISP in India
   i. Microsoft ☐ ii. Airtel ☐ iii. Google ☐

d. A single page on the internet
   i. Website ☐ ii. Web Page ☐ iii. Web browser ☐

e. A software which provides all the information present on the Web site
   i. URL ☐ ii. Web browser ☐ iii. Home page ☐

4. Write 'T' for true and 'F' for false in the boxes:

a. The Internet is a collection of different networks. ☐

b. A Web page is a single page on the Internet. ☐

c. There is no need for an ISP for an Internet connection. ☐

d. On the Internet, you can play many different types of online games. ☐

e. The Internet is the biggest means of communication. ☐

f. The address of a Web page or Website is called Home page. ☐

g. You cannot do shopping through the Internet. ☐

5. Fill in the blanks:

a. The Internet can be described as a __________ of __________.

b. __________ allows you to exchange the typed messages with another person on the Internet.

c. Many companies make their __________ on the Internet to advertise their products.

d. __________ is a device that connects the computer with telephone lines.

e. __________ is a video sharing service.

f. __________ is the first page of a Website.

6. Give the full forms of the following:

a. WWW __________

b. ISP __________

c. Modem __________

d. URL __________

LAB ACTIVITY

- **In the computer lab, watch carefully the devices required for the Internet connection and write the names of those devices.**
- **Open the Website of your school and write down the URL of your school Website.**

Formative Assessment-4
(Chapters 8-9)

1. Complete the Repeat command to draw a:

a. Square

Repeat ___ [___ 50 RT ___]

b. Pentagon

Repeat ___ [FD ___ RT ___]

c. Semi-Circle

Repeat ___ [FD ___ RT 1]

d. Hexagon

Repeat ___ [FD 50 RT ___]

e. Triangle

Repeat ___ [___ 50 ___ ___]

2. Match the following. One has been done for your help:

a.		• Internet
b.		• Chatting
c.		• Modem
d.		• Computer
e.		• Video sharing platform
f.		• ISP

Summative Assessment-2
(Chapters 5-9)

1. Tick (✓) the correct answers:

a. The picture position that displays multiple copies of the image repeated

i. Center ☐ ii. Tile ☐ iii. Stretch ☐

b. A moving image that appears when the computer remains untouched for some time

i. Background ☐ ii. Screen saver ☐ iii. Desktop ☐

c. The plain area within the Word window where the text is typed

i. Work Area ☐ ii. Scroll bar ☐ iii. Ribbon ☐

d. The bar on the left corner of the title bar is

i. Control bar ☐ ii. Ribbon ☐

iii. Quick Access Toolbar ☐

e. Toolbar used to get quick access to common formatting commands

i. Mini toolbar ☐ ii. Anti-virus ☐ iii. WordArt ☐

f. Changing and arranging text in a document to make it attractive

i. Editing ☐ ii. Formatting ☐ iii. Writing ☐

g. The triangle-shaped object in LOGO screen

i. Square ☐ ii. Turtle ☐ iii. Mouse ☐

2. Fill in the blanks:

a. __________ is a combination of background, colour scheme, screen saver and sound.

b. A word processor is an __________ software program that enables you to type your text in a computer.

c. __________ is a Word processor software produced by IBM.

d. The Ribbon consists a __________ of tabs.

e. You can assign ____________ or ____________ notation to any text to make it appear above or below the regular line of text.

f. ____________ is a video sharing service.

3. Write 'T' for true and 'F' for false in the boxes:.

a. Gadgets are the programs that appear on the right side of the desktop. ☐

b. A Word processor is formally known as document preparation system. ☐

c. Backstage view has three panels. ☐

d. MS-Word 2016 is the latest version of Microsoft Word. ☐

e. Forward command brings the turtle in backward direction. ☐

f. PRINT Command is used to display anything on the LOGO screen. ☐

g. The Internet is a worldwide system of computers. ☐

h. You cannot chat on the Internet. ☐

4. Answer the following questions:

a. What is a screen saver?

b. What is the need for personalizing a desktop?

c. Explain the components of MS-Word 2016 Window.

d. Why do you need to select text?

e. Name two word processing programs.

f. What is the use of mini toolbar?

g. What is the use of superscript or subscript in MS-Word?

h. Explain the five Text cases in Word.

i. What is the use of copy formatting text?

j. What is the use of Repeat command in LOGO?

k. What is the use of Print command in LOGO?

l. What is the Internet? Explain its uses.

m. What is the use of hyperlink?

PROJECT WORK

MS-WORD

Write an essay on 'My Country' in the space provided below:

MY COUNTRY

- Now open MS-Word and type the above lines in a new document.
- Write the title of text through WordArt feature.
- The paragraph font should be 'Arial' and font size be 14.
- Now save the file with the name 'My Country'.
- Close the file and exit from MS-Word program.

INTERNET

Gain access to the Internet and open the sites related to the topic 'cricket'.

Collect the different pieces of information. If possible, try to copy and paste the information in MS-Word document and save the document file as 'cricket'.

10 Let's Learn Coding in Scratch

Hello children! Today I'm going to tell you about a new program "Scratch" which is designed to be full of fun, educational and easy to learn. It has the tools for creating interactive stories, games, art simulations and using block-based programming. Let us know more about this program.

A scratch is a free multimedia programming language that uses codes to create interactive stories, games, animations, music and art by simple dragging and dropping of instructions. It is a programming tool that can be used by students, teachers, scholars and parents for Science and Maths projects, presentations, simulation, experiments, etc.

Do you remember Scratchjr Program you learnt in the previous class?

Yes, we remember how we used coding in making our story.

Scratch is a program used to create interactive stories, animations, games, etc. It helps us to learn and think creatively, systematically as well as work collaboratively. Scratch is a block-based visual programming language. This program was developed by the MIT media lab, and it is provided free of cost.

Note

We are using Scratch 3.12. You can download Scratch 3.12 from this link: https://scratch.mit.edu/download

To open Scratch, follow the given steps:

1. Click start button.

2. Scroll the menu and select scratch3.

The following window will appear on the computer. Now, let's learn about the different parts of Scratch window.

There are four main elements in the Scratch window.

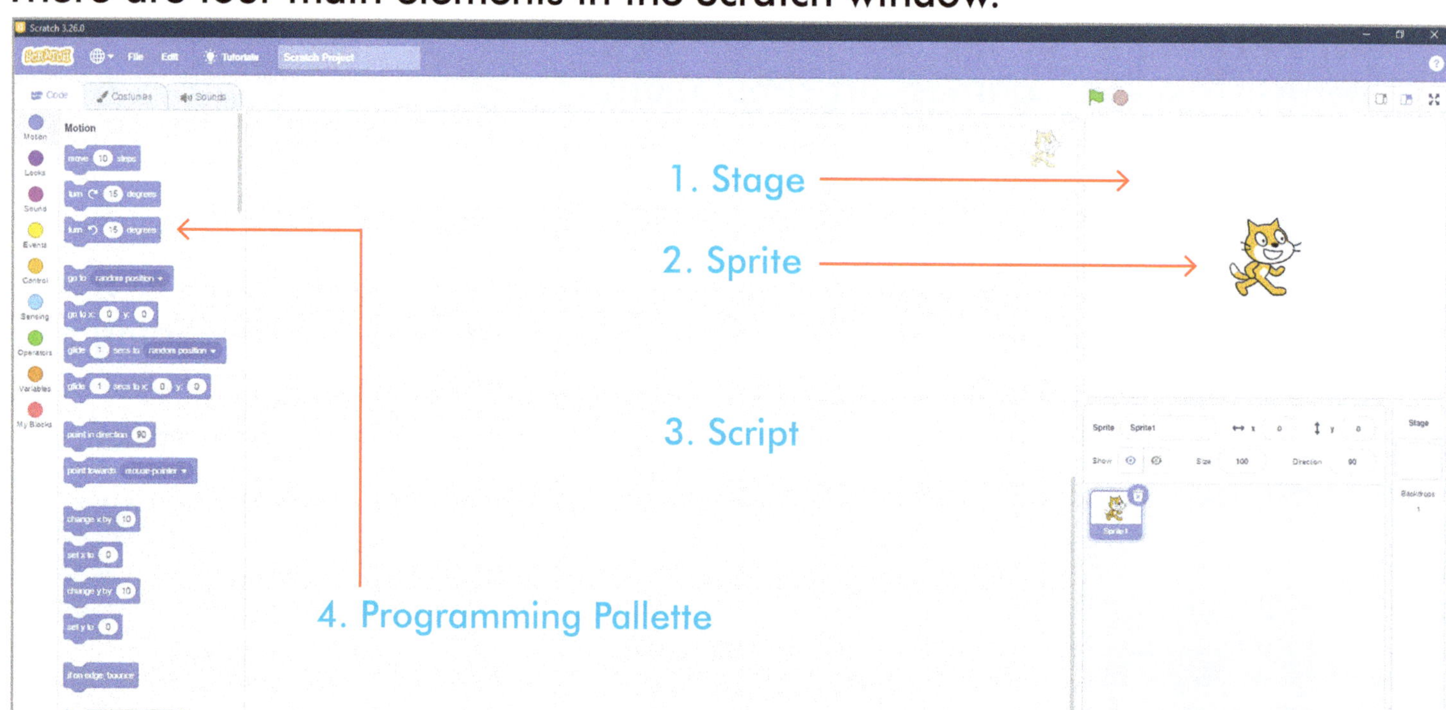

1. **Stage :** It is place where all the action takes place. We can add different backgrounds on the stage.
2. **Sprite :** It is a character on the stage that performs all the actions. We can add as many characters as we like on the stage.
3. **Script :** It is the place where all the programming is done with the help of the programming blocks. To program a sprite we need to click and drag the programming blocks in the Script area.

Do you know

'Pac-Man' Game

Pac-Man game was very popular in the 1980s and 1990s and is still played worldwide. By playing it perfectly, without losing any life, and completing all 255 levels, one can achieve 3,333,360 points.

4. **Programming palette :** It is the area where all the programming blocks are available. These programming blocks are divided into different sections, such as Motions, Looks, Sound, etc.

Now, as we know the different parts of scratch, we can start coding.

Test your Progress...

Label the parts of the Scratch 3.12 window.

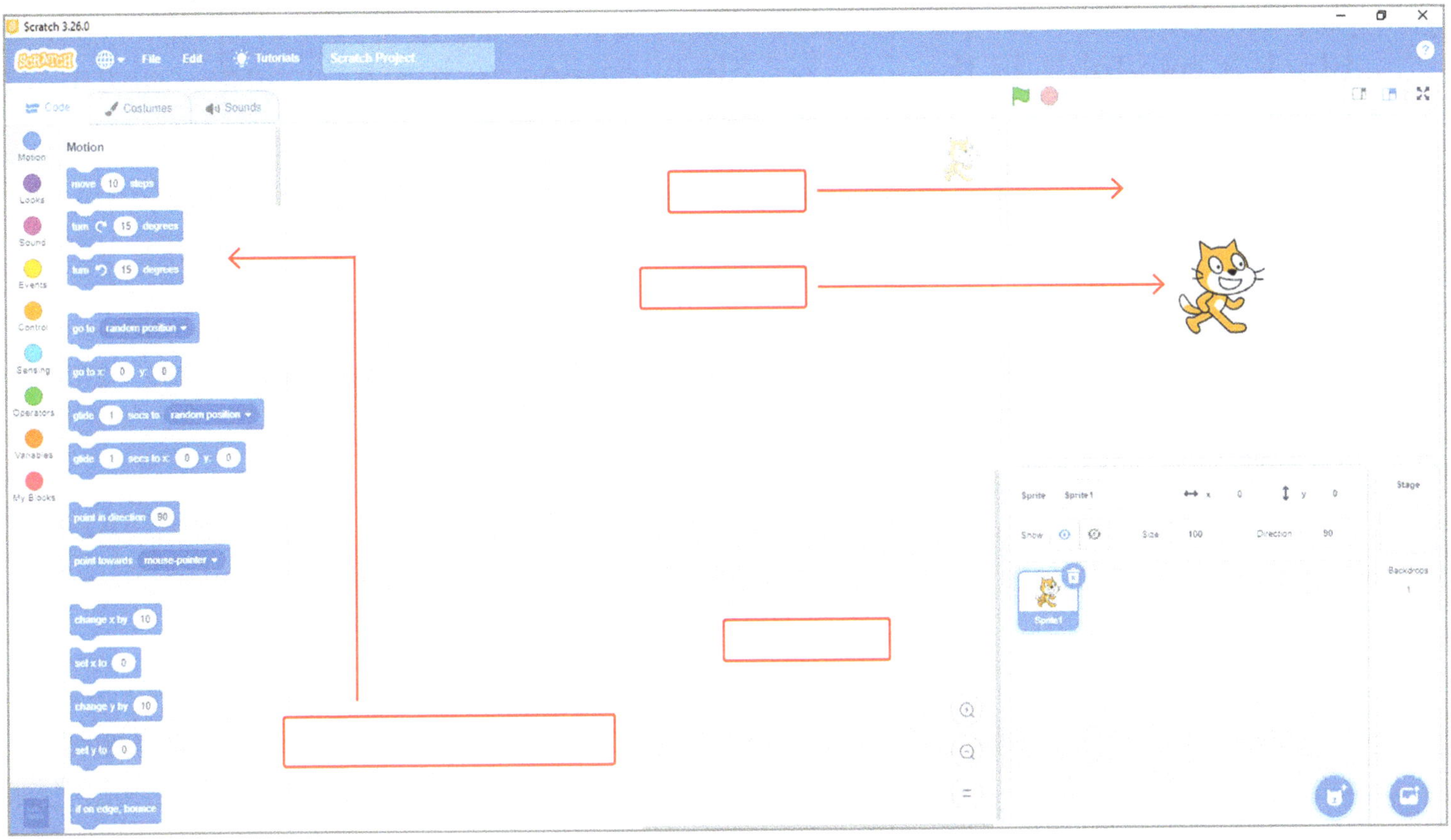

Project : Make the Sprite dance in Scratch 3.12

Now, let us create a program to make the sprite dance in scratch. We will use Looks, Motion, Control and Sound blocks to complete this project.

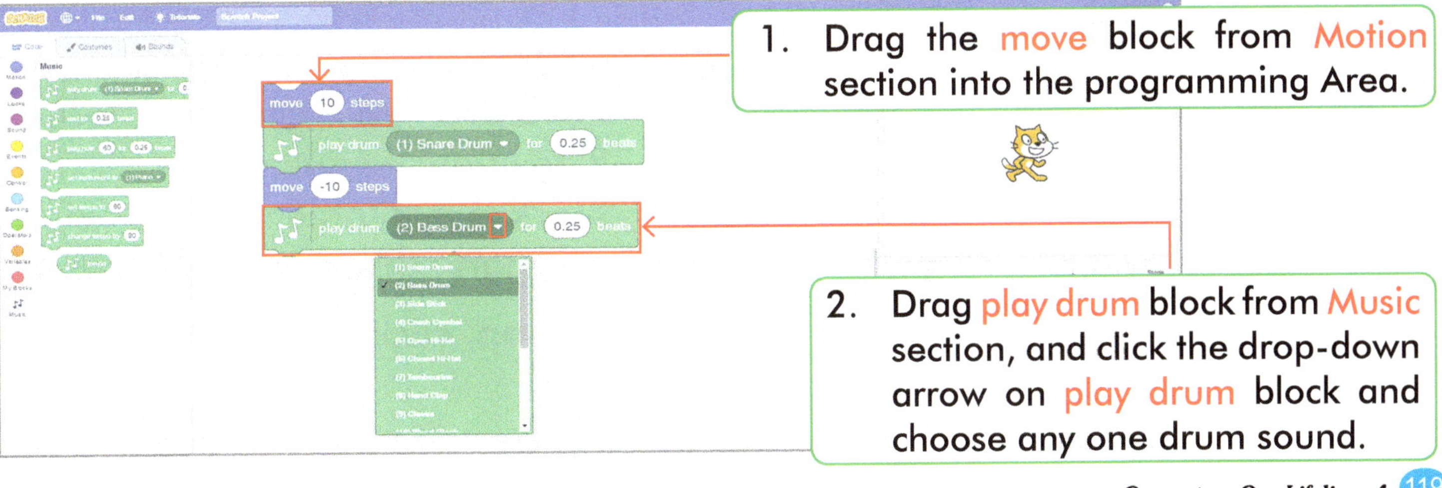

1. Drag the move block from Motion section into the programming Area.

2. Drag play drum block from Music section, and click the drop-down arrow on play drum block and choose any one drum sound.

- ⇒ The Motion block category is in Cyan (light blue) colour. It contains different blocks to make the sprite move, turn, go to, etc.
- ⇒ To open the Music Block category, click on the ( ) button on the down left corner of the scratch window and select Music from the options available.

Now, the cat will move and play the drum, but it plays the drum once. *Don't you want to make it move and play the drum continuously?*

- ⇒ Repeat block — It helps to repeat the blocks coding again and again. This block is available in the Control block category; it is in orange colour.

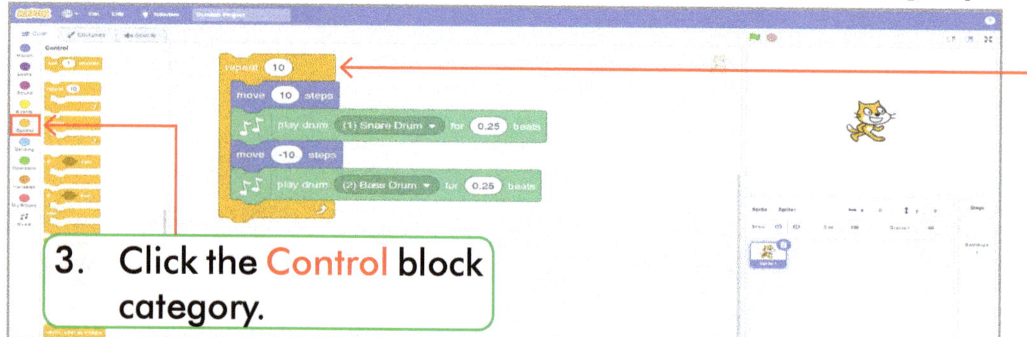

3. Click the Control block category.
4. Drag out a repeat block and drop it on top of the stack. The mouth of the repeat should wrap around the other blocks.

Now, make the Sprite Speak something

To make the sprite to say anything on the stage we use say block. It helps the sprite to say anything in callouts; this block is available in the Looks category; it is in blue colour.

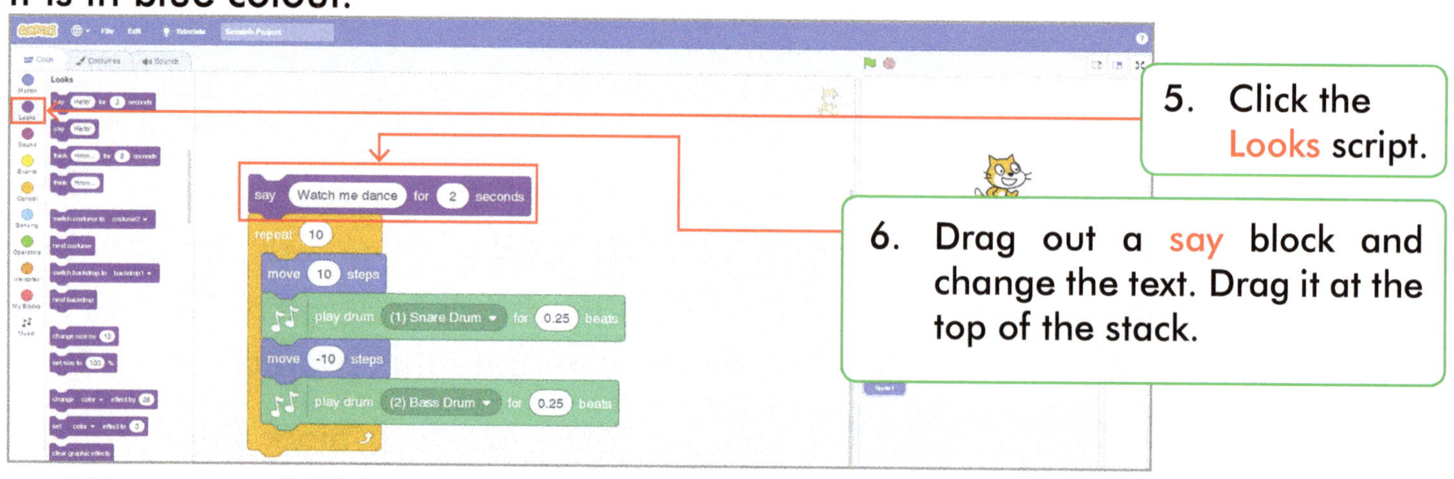

5. Click the Looks script.
6. Drag out a say block and change the text. Drag it at the top of the stack.

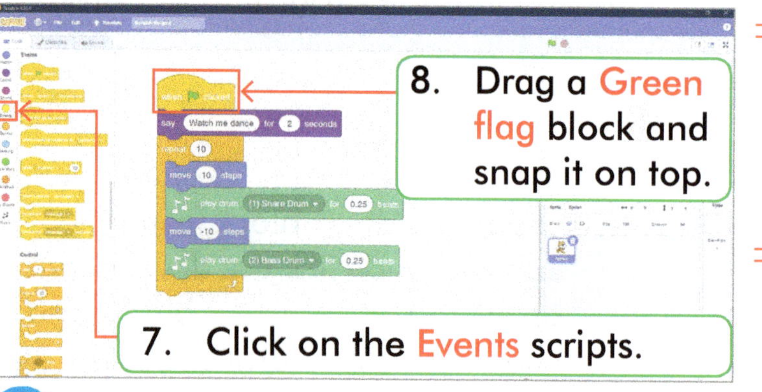

7. Click on the Events scripts.
8. Drag a Green flag block and snap it on top.

- ⇒ Wherever you click the Green Flag, your script will start. This block is available in Events block category; this is yellow in colour.
- ⇒ To stop, click the stop button .

Let us change the colour of the cat alternately when it is being animated.

9. Click on the Looks block category.

10. Drag out a change effect by block.

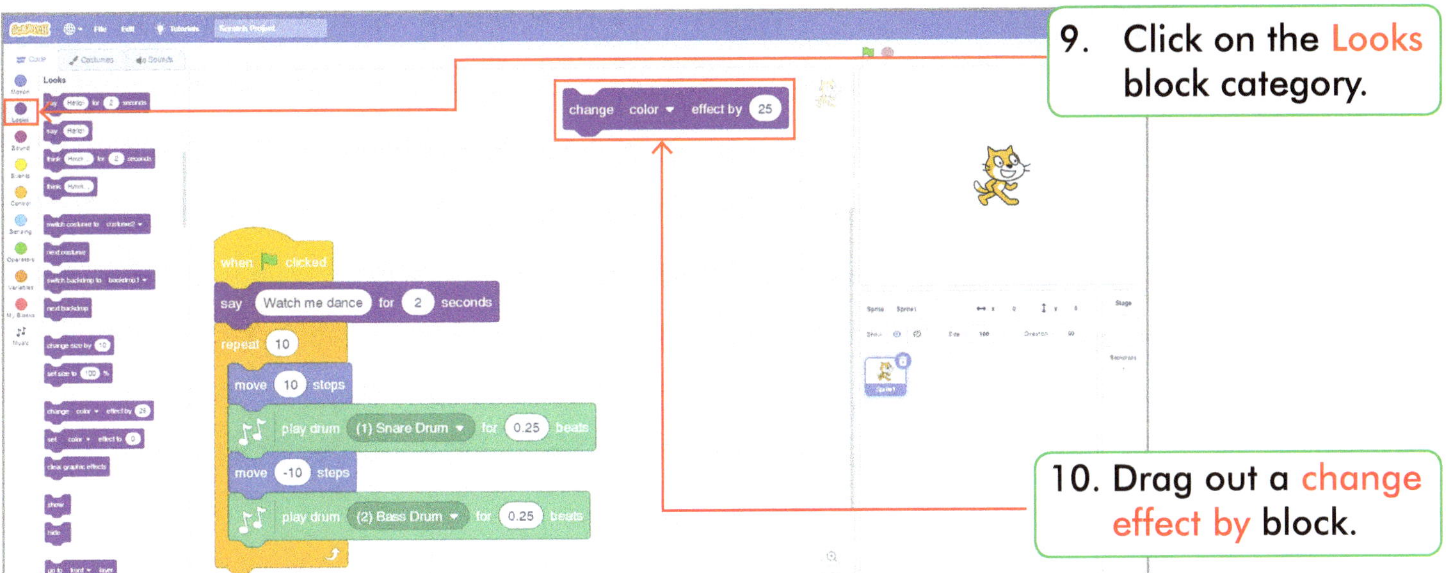

⇒ To control the change of the colour of the cat with the press of any key on the keyboard, you can drag the When key pressed block from the Events category.

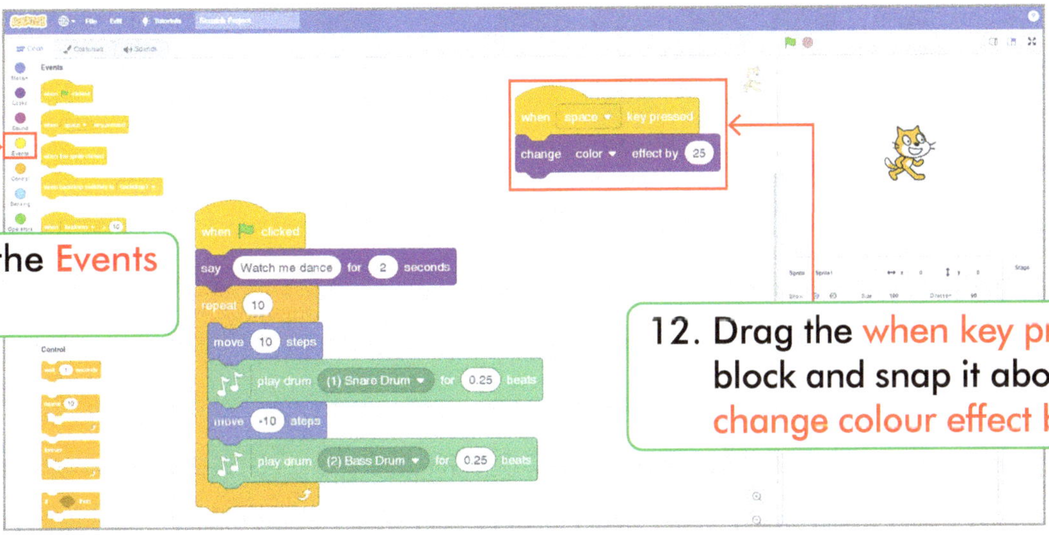

11. Click on the Events category.

12. Drag the when key pressed block and snap it above change colour effect by block.

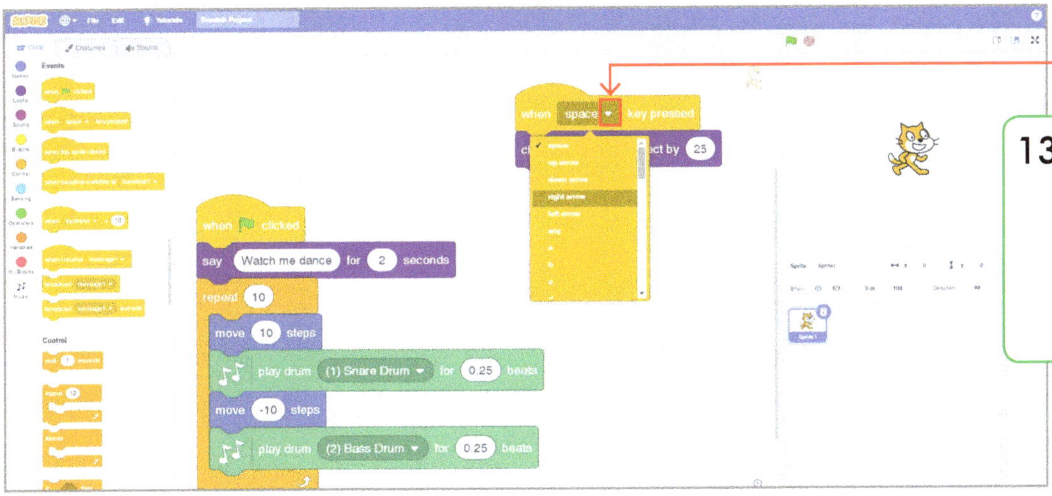

13. Click the drop-down arrow on when key pressed block and select any key of your choice.

We can also add a backdrop to the stage. To change the background we have to click on the background button on the right down corner of the window.

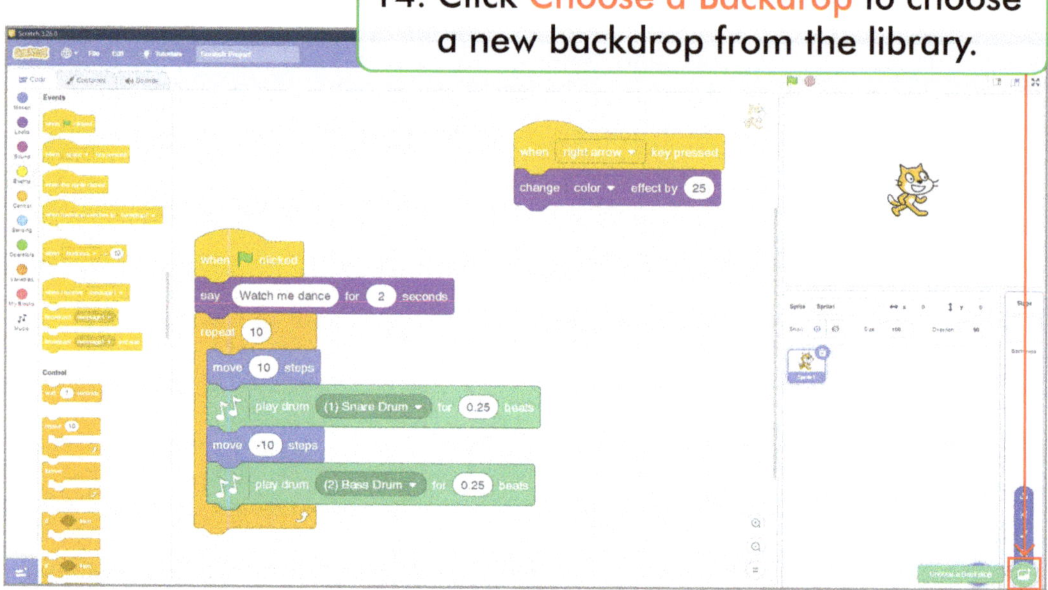

14. Click Choose a Backdrop to choose a new backdrop from the library.

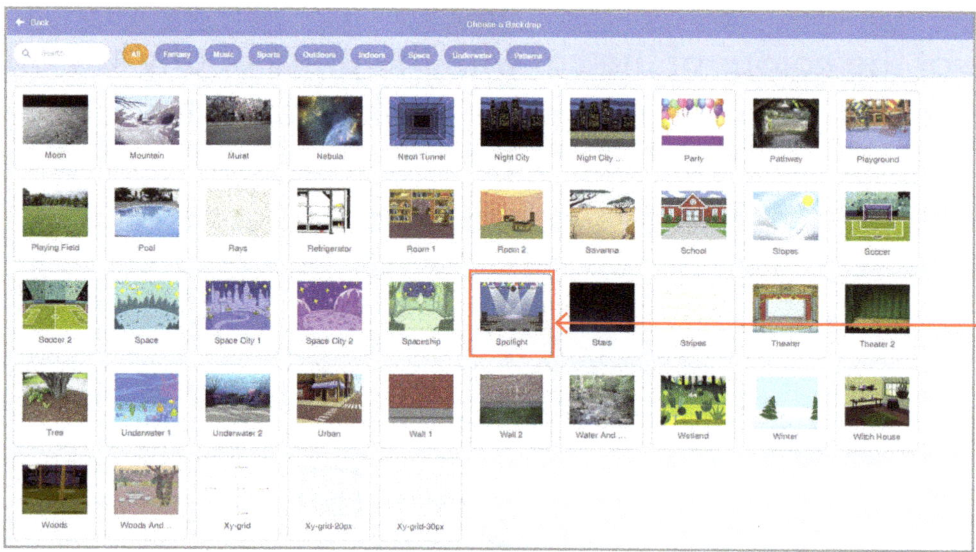

15. Select any backdrop and click on it.

Let's Add More Character on the Stage

We can add n number of characters on the stage. To add more character, click on the choose a sprite button on the right down corner of the stage.

The following are the different sprite buttons.

New Sprite Buttons are:

- Choose a sprite
- Paint your own sprite
- Surprise
- Upload your own image or sprite

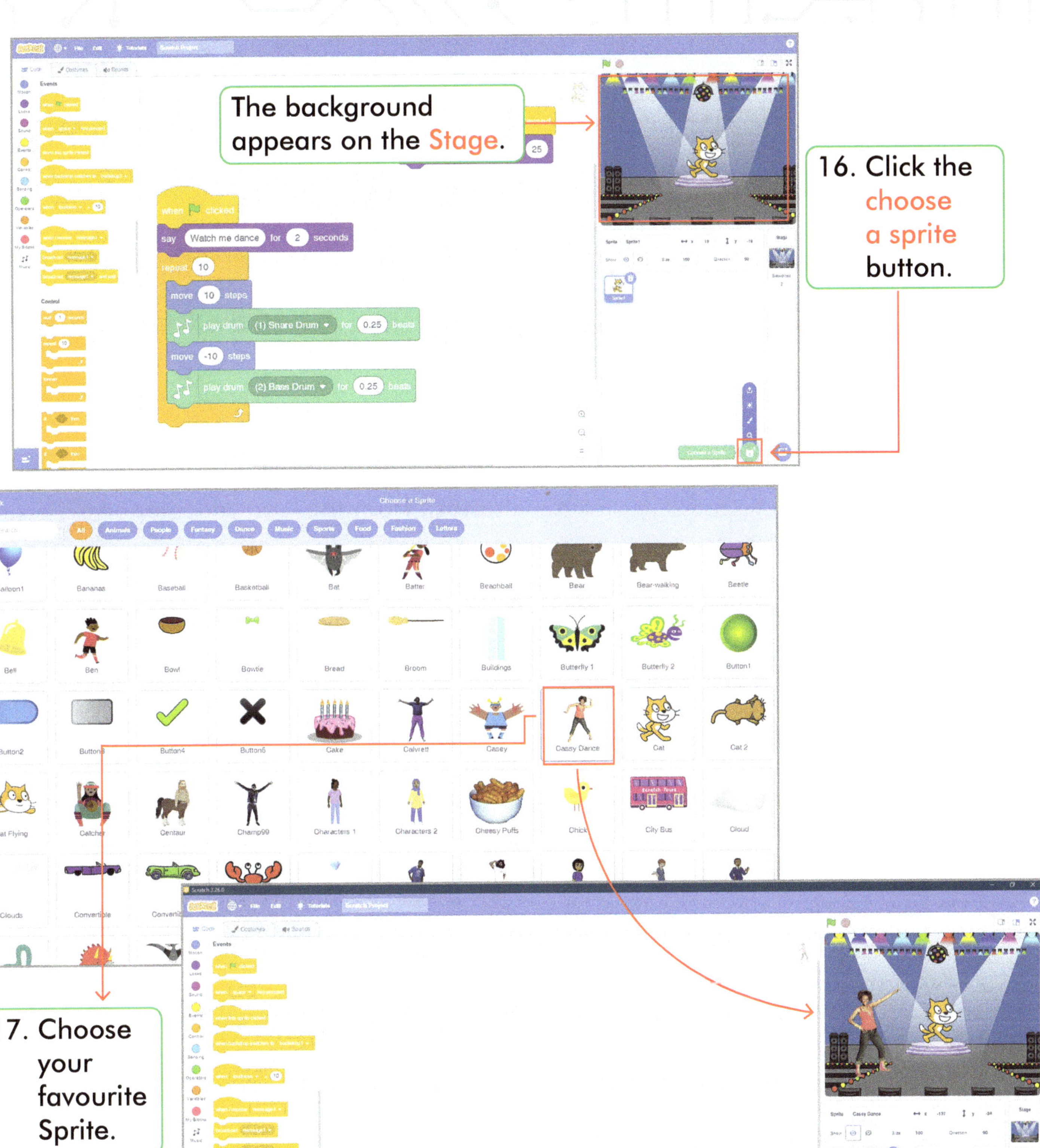

Let's animate the new sprite by switching between costumes. So, let us create a programming script for the new sprite.

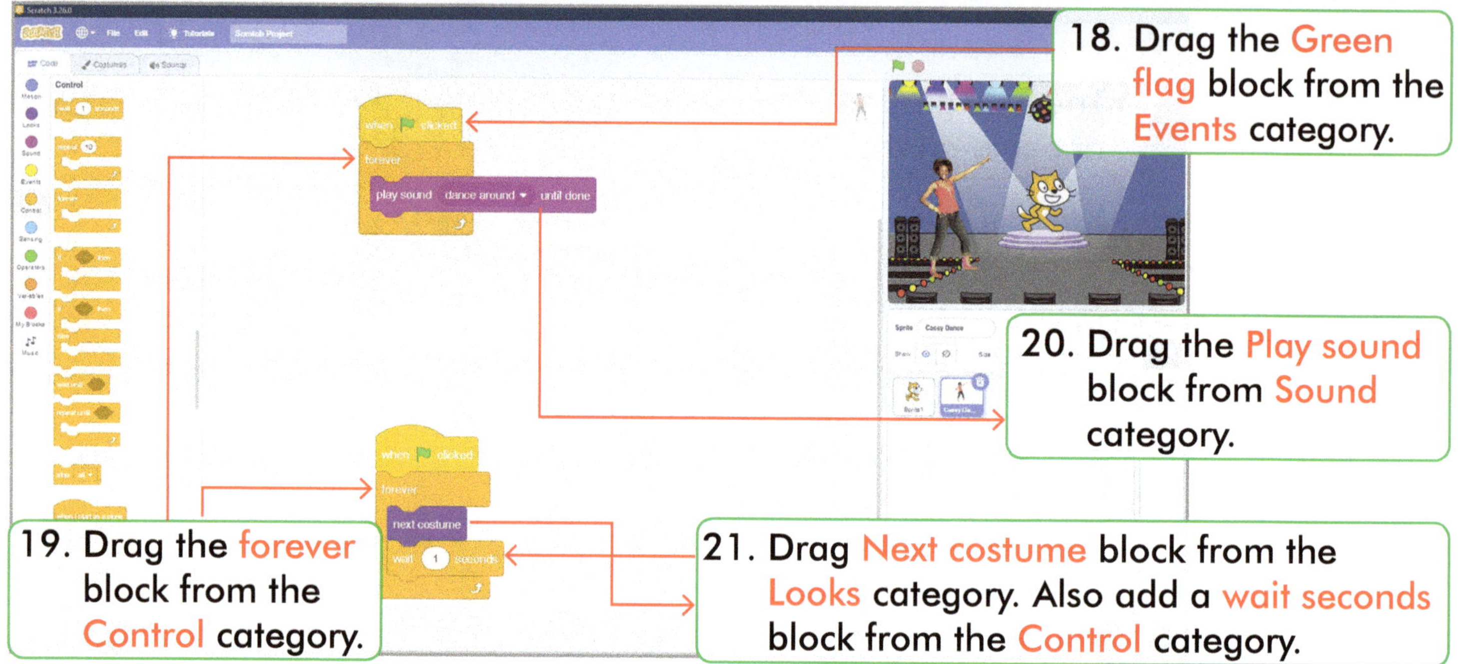

Note

Wait block helps to see the change in the costume, otherwise the change is so fast that you won't be able to see the changes, and it won't look like animated.

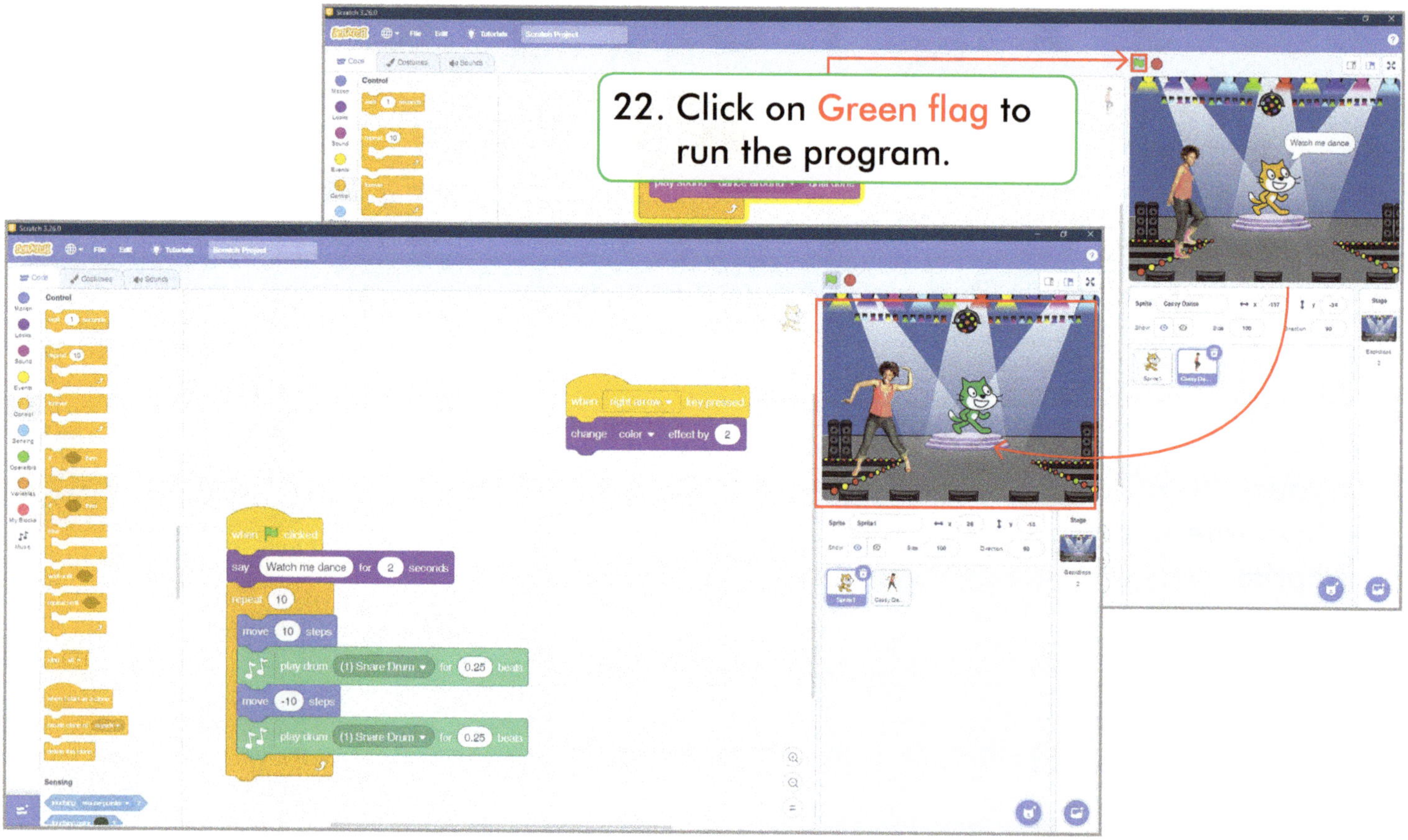

22. Click on Green flag to run the program.

Did you enjoy the dance? Now you should save your project for the future. Also, you can share it with your friends or online community of scratch.

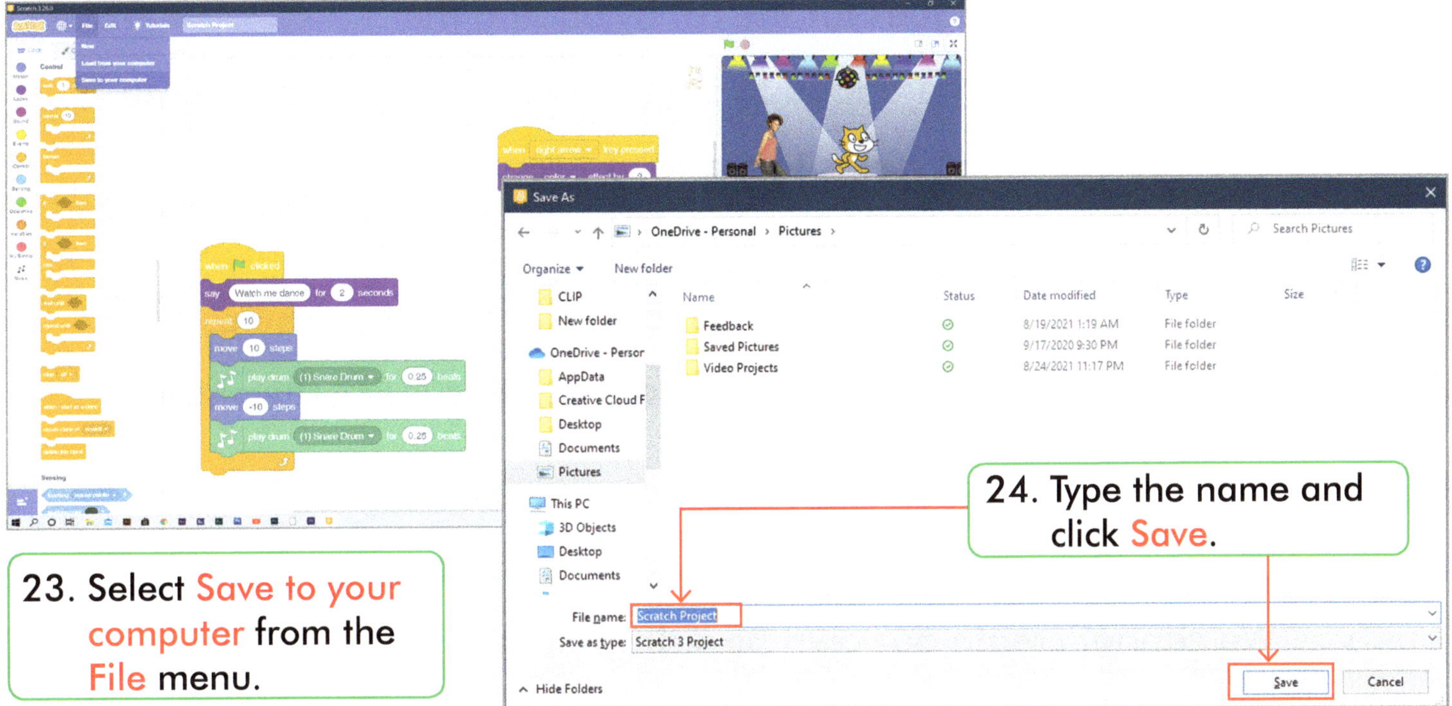
23. Select Save to your computer from the File menu.

24. Type the name and click Save.

LET'S HAVE A LOOK

- Scratch 3.12 helps us to make our own interactive stories, games, and animations.
- Repeat block is available in the Control category which helps to repeat the action as many number of times as we wish.
- The Say block is available in the Looks category which helps to display any dialogue.
- Flag block is available in Events category and helps to execute the program by clicking on the green flag and stop the program by clicking on the stop button.
- Change colour block is available in Looks category helps to change the colour of the Sprite.
- The When key pressed block is available in Control category which helps the Sprite to execute the statements when the specified key is pressed.
- There are four types of new sprite buttons.
- Next costume block is available in Looks category which helps to switch between the different postures or costumes.

BRAIN TEASER

1. Fill in the blank.

Stop, Green, Say, Repeat, New Sprite, Backdrop, Forever

a. We can make the cat dance 10 times by adding the ____________ block.

b. We can add dialogues for the cat by adding the __________ block.

c. Background can be added to stage from __________ menu.

d. __________ flag helps to start the program.

e. __________ button stops the program.

f. __________ block helps to execute the program endlessly.

g. __________ button helps to add more Sprites to the stage.

2. Write 'T' for true and 'F' for false in the boxes:

a. We can make the cat dance 30 times by forever block. ☐

b. We cannot create our own backdrop or Sprite. ☐

c. The cat stops dancing if the stop button is clicked. ☐

d. Any sprite can change its costume from the Event Script. ☐

e. The cat can say "How are you?" by the Repeat block. ☐

f. The Green flag can be added from the Event Script. ☐

3. Answer the following questions.

a. Write briefly about all the four elements of the Scratch window:

i. Stage : __________

____

ii. Sprite : __________

____

iii. Programming palette : __________

____

iv. Script : __________

____

b. Write the name of the four new Sprite buttons.

____

c. How can we add a new backdrop to the stage?

____

d. Number the given blocks in the correct order to form a conversation.

Now create this script in Scratch for the cat Sprite.

e. Your teacher has assigned a task to create a project on the topic Yoga and its benefits in Scratch. You have to add music to the project. Which blocks will you use?

Match the colours of the different action block categories.

Motion Scripts	▪	▪	(purple)
Events Scripts	▪	▪	(pink)
Looks Scripts	▪	▪	(blue)
Sound Scripts	▪	▪	(yellow)

For Teachers:

- **Help the students to open scratch 3.12 window.**
- **Explain to the students about drag & drop the block in the programming area.**

- **Help the students to explore the changes that can be done with each of the blocks.**

For Students:

- **Develop a coir of starfish using underwater backdrop. Each starfish plays a different drum when the keys of the keyboard are pressed.**
- **Develop a project to animate your name.**

The steps are:

- Choose the First Letter
- Add Colour Effect and play Drum
- Add a Backdrop
- Make it spin
- Go on adding letters and making it spin or change its colour.

```
when [flag] clicked
change color ▾ effect by (25)
play drum ((2) Bass Drum ▾) for (0.25) beats
```

```
when [flag] clicked
play drum ((7) Tambourine ▾) for (0.25) beats
repeat (15)
    turn ↻ (15) degrees
    wait (1) seconds
↺
```

www.ingramcontent.com/pod-product-compliance
Ingram Content Group UK Ltd.
Pitfield, Milton Keynes, MK11 3LW, UK
UKHW050144280726
14058UKWH00006B/814

9 788131 016428